Ultimate
Italian Cookbook

Step by Step Guide to 111 Easy and Delicious Italian Recipes

by
Slavka Bodic

Introduction

Italian cuisine is one of the most popular in the world, which you will find served not only in restaurants but also cooked at home. No matter where you come from, you are most likely familiar with Italian dishes such as pizza, spaghetti Bolognese or tortellini, among others. However, more dishes complement superb Italian cuisine such as meat, desserts, and soups.

This cookbook consists of 111 recipes that are easy to make, healthy but also tasty. All recipes are either with very few ingredients or very easy to make. In some cases, where cooking with a slow cooker is suggested, cooking time is a bit longer, but recipes are still simple and delicious. I decided to fully exclude the most famous Italian dish – pizza, since making homemade pizza is art per se and it deserves a cookbook of its own!

The Italian dishes in this cookbook consist mainly of wheat products, such as pasta and bread, vegetables, meat cheese and fish. Most of the ingredients used are can be found in any country. Apart from adjustments related to ingredients, I tried to use the simplest forms of cooking techniques such as boiling, pan-frying, browning, roasting, baking and grilling.

This cookbook is arranged in sections ranging from breakfast, main dishes, desserts, appetizers and dips, pastries, salads and soups. The selected recipes are mostly modern takes on traditional dishes or something that you can eat in beautiful Italian restaurants in this amazing country.

At the moment, you can check my Balkan Cookbook, Greek Cookbook, Serbian Cookbook, Turkish Cookbook, Persian Cookbook, Armenian Cookbook, as well as 111 recipes for your Mediterranean diet. All books are available in different formats on Amazon.

Why Italian Cuisine?

When we are talking about Italian cuisine, we are talking about more than 20 cuisines. Up until 150 years ago, Italy was divided. There were 27 different regions, each with its own customs, traditions, dialects, cuisine and favorite ingredients. Even today, it is quite hard to define dishes that are relevant for the entire country. Tuscany became famous for its excellent bread, while Naples is the birthplace of pizza with tomatoes. There is a common belief that Marco Polo brought pasta to Italy, but there is no hard evidence for this story. Moreover, people in some regions like Lombardy were hardly eating any pasta and they used polenta instead.

The big migration of Italians happened before the First World War and shortly after the Second World War. Their eating habits spread quickly all around the world, especially given that all their dishes were quite easy to make. Ingredients were available everywhere and the dishes were delicious.

A typical Italian meal always start with *Antipasti* – selection of snacks (meat, cheese, olives, vegetable), served with an alcohol. The next one is *Primo piatto* and this part of meal could be a small portion of paste, soup, risotto or gnocchi. *Secondo piatto* typically includes meat (poultry, fish, veal, beef or lamb). However, *secodno* is not always the most important part of the meal. That depends on the region. *Formagi e Frutta* is the next one dedicated to local cheese selection and peeled fruits, followed by *Dolce* where delicious deserts, and followed by *Espresso e digestivo* at the end.

All meals are quite "open" and experiments with an increase in the amount of some ingredients or the addition of entirely new spices or vegetables is always considered a good option!

Table of Contents

Just in case ...

Cooking Measurement Chart

Weight

imperial	metric
1/2 oz	15 g
1 oz	29 g
2 oz	57 g
3 oz	85 g
4 oz	113 g
5 oz	141 g
6 oz	170 g
8 oz	227 g
10 oz	283 g
12 oz	340 g
13 oz	369 g
14 oz	397 g
15 oz	425 g
1 lb	453 g

Measurement

cup	onces	milliliters	tbsp.
8 cup	64 oz	1895 ml	128
6 cup	48 oz	1420 ml	96
5 cup	40 oz	1180 ml	80
4 cup	32 oz	960 ml	64
2 cup	16 oz	480 ml	32
1 cup	8 oz	240 ml	16
3/4 cup	6 oz	177 ml	12
2/3 cup	5 oz	158 ml	11
1/2 cup	4 oz	118 ml	8
3/8 cup	3 oz	90 ml	6
1/3 cup	2.5 oz	79 ml	5.5
1/4 cup	2 oz	59 ml	4
1/8 cup	1 oz	30 ml	3
1/16 cup	1/2 oz	15 ml	1

Temperature

fahrenheit	celsius
100 °F	37 °C
150 °F	65 °C
200 °F	93 °C
250 °F	121 °C
300 °F	150 °C
325 °F	160 °C
350 °F	180 °C
375 °F	190 °C
400 °F	200 °C
425 °F	220 °C
450 °F	230 °C
500 °F	260 °C
525 °F	274 °C
550 °F	288 °C

Breakfast

Italian Baked Sausage and Eggs

Preparation time: 15 minutes

Cooking time: 30 minutes

Nutrition facts (per serving): 408 Cal (fats 11g, proteins 19g, fibers 3g)

Ingredients (8 servings)

1 pound of Italian sausage

24 Oz of roasted tomato and garlic pasta sauce

A can of diced tomatoes, drained

8 eggs

¼ teaspoon of pepper

¼ teaspoon of salt

¾ cup of part-skim ricotta cheese

Some basil leaves

¼ cup of shredded parmesan cheese

¼ cup of softened butter

1 tablespoon of minced basil

1 (4 Oz) French bread demi-baguette, cut into 1-inch slices

Preparation

Preheat the oven to 350 F. Cook the sausage in a skillet until it is no longer pink and drain. Stir in the pasta sauce and tomatoes. Transfer the mixture into a baking dish and dollop the ricotta cheese on it. Break the eggs into a bowl and slip them gently into the ricotta. Sprinkle with pepper, salt and parmesan cheese and bake for 27-32 minutes, or until the egg yolks begin to thicken. Sprinkle with some basil and set aside. Spread the butter on the bread slices and place them on an ungreased baking sheet. Broil them on a preheated grill for about 4 minutes and serve them immediately with the baked eggs.

Sausage Veggie Strata

Preparation time: 15 minutes
Cooking time: 90 minutes
Nutrition facts (per serving): 501 Cal (fats 34g, proteins 27g, fibers 2g)

Ingredients (6 servings)

1 pound of Italian sausage
1 green capsicum, chopped
½ of a medium-sized onion, chopped
4 eggs
1 cup of shredded Swiss cheese
5 Oz of frozen spinach, thawed, dried and chopped
½ of a medium-sized zucchini, cut into ¼-inch slices
1 cup of milk
1 teaspoon of ground mustard
1 teaspoon of salt
6 slices of bread, cut into ½-inch pieces
1 teaspoon of white pepper
1 cup of shredded cheddar cheese

Preparation

Heat a skillet over a medium heat; add in the sausage, capsicum and onions. Cook until the meat is no longer pink. Drain and set aside. Whisk the eggs, salt, pepper, milk and mustard into a bowl. Stir in the sausage mixture, cheese, zucchini, spinach and bread. Put it into a baking dish, cover and refrigerate overnight. Let it sit for about 30 minutes before baking. Bake at 350 F for 45 minutes, or until cooked through.

Jalapeno Pepper Frittata

Preparation time: 10 minutes

Cooking time: 20 minutes

Nutrition facts (per serving): 201 Cal (fats 10g, proteins 17g, fibers 2g)

Ingredients (4 servings)

5 eggs

1 garlic clove, minced

1 medium-sized onion, chopped

1 jalapeno pepper, chopped and seeded

1 medium green capsicum, chopped

1 medium red capsicum, chopped

1 tablespoon of olive oil

1/8 teaspoon of pepper

½ teaspoon of salt

1 ¼ cups of egg substitute

1 tablespoon of grated Romano cheese

Preparation

In a bowl, whisk the eggs, cheese, egg substitute, salt and pepper. Heat the oil in a skillet over a medium-high heat. Add the capsicum and onions in and cook. Stir until tender. Add the garlic and cook for 1 minute more. Add the egg mixture in and cook while covered for about 11-12 minutes, or until set. Cut into wedges and serve.

Italian Mushroom Frittata Stack

Preparation time: 25 minutes
Cooking time: 20 minutes
Nutrition facts (per serving): 468 Cal (fats 44g, proteins 17g, fibers 1g)

Ingredients (6 servings)

8 eggs
¾ pound of sliced mushrooms
8 Oz of mascarpone cheese
1/3 cup of heavy whipping cream
1/8 teaspoon of pepper
2 garlic cloves, minced
2 tablespoons of minced basil
½ cup of grated Romano cheese
5 tablespoons of olive oil
1 medium-sized onion, thinly sliced
1 ½ teaspoons of salt

Preparation

Into a bowl, whisk the cream, eggs, ¼ cup of Romano cheese and 1 teaspoon of salt. Heat 2 tablespoons of oil in a skillet over a medium-high heat. Add the onions and mushrooms and cook stirring until tender. Stir in the garlic, salt and pepper, cook for a couple of minutes and transfer into a bowl. Stir in the remaining Romano and mascarpone cheese and set aside. In a skillet, heat 1 tablespoon of oil, pour in 2/3 cup of the egg mixture and cook until it sets to make frittatas. Repeat with the rest of the egg mixture to make two more frittatas. To serve, place the frittata on a plate, add a layer of the mushroom mixture and repeat with the other two frittatas, then cut and serve.

Zucchini Ham Italian Quiche

Preparation time: 15 minutes
Cooking time: 50 minutes
Nutrition facts (per serving): 310 Cal (fats 17g, proteins 22g, fibers 1g)

Ingredients (4 servings)
$^1/_3$ cup of whole purpose flour
1 cup of grated cheddar cheese
3 green onions
1 ½ cups of milk
1 medium-sized zucchini, coarsely chopped
3 eggs
3 slices of ham, coarsely chopped
2 tablespoons of finely chopped parsley leaves

Preparation
Into a bowl, whisk the milk, eggs and flour until smooth and stir in the rest of the ingredients. Bake the mixture for about 45 minutes at a temperature of 350 F. Sprinkle the parsley and serve.

Italian Egg Toast

Preparation time: 5 minutes

Cooking time: 5 minutes

Nutrition facts (per serving): 185 Cal (fats 6g, proteins 14g, fibers 3g)

Ingredients (2 servings)

½ cup of pizza sauce

2 slices of bread

2 eggs

1 ½ tablespoons of olive oil

4 tablespoons of shredded mozzarella cheese

Some Italian seasonings

Preparation

Heat the pizza sauce in a skillet and set aside. Heat the oil in a skillet, crack in the eggs and cook until the whites are set. Toast the bread slices, divide the pizza sauce, cheese, and eggs on each toast.

Italian Poached Eggs

Preparation time: 5 minutes
Cooking time: 7 minutes
Nutrition facts (per serving): 145 Cal (fats 12.2g, proteins 7.2g, fibers 1g)

Ingredients (4 servings)

2 tablespoons of olive oil

14 Oz of tomatoes with herbs, diced

¼ teaspoon of minced garlic cloves

1 tablespoon of freshly chopped rosemary

A dash of red pepper flakes

1 tablespoon of freshly chopped parsley

2 tablespoons of grated parmesan cheese

4 eggs

Preparation

Heat the oil in a skillet, add the parsley, tomatoes, garlic and rosemary and bring to a boil. Simmer for about 5-6 minutes and stir in the pepper flakes. Make four hollows and crack an egg in each space. Cover and cook until they are done. Scoop the eggs with sauce on a plate and garnish with cheese and parsley.

Vanilla Laced Tiramisu Crepes

Preparation time: 60 minutes

Cooking time: 5 minutes

Nutrition facts (per serving): 234 Cal (fats 15.1g, proteins 2.2g, fibers 0.3g)

Ingredients (22 crepes)

4 eggs

2 tablespoons of brewed coffee

¼ cup of club soda

¾ cup of milk

3 tablespoons of melted butter

1 tablespoon of vanilla extract

1 cup of all-purpose flour

¼ teaspoon of salt

2 tablespoons of baking cocoa

3 tablespoons of sugar

Filling

2 tablespoons of vanilla extract

8 Oz of mascarpone cheese

1 cup of sugar

¼ cup of brewed coffee

8 Oz of softened cream cheese

Some whipped cream and cocoa

Preparation

Into a bowl, whisk the milk, butter, eggs, coffee, vanilla, baking soda and salt. Cover and keep refrigerated for 55-65 minutes. Heat a nonstick skillet over a medium heat and add two tablespoons of batter in, tilt to coat the pan evenly and cook both sides for about 30 seconds. Repeat the process with the remaining batter. Cool and stack the crepes with paper towels in-between.

Make the filling

Add the cheese and sugar into a bowl, beat until fluffy and stir the vanilla extract in. Place 2 tablespoons of the mixture on each crepe and roll them up. Top with whipped cream and cocoa.

Brunch Bake

Preparation time: 30 minutes
Cooking time: 55 minutes
Nutrition facts (per serving): 373 Cal (fats 20g, proteins 24g, fibers 3g)

Ingredients (12 servings)

12 eggs
1 pound of Italian sausage
1 onion, chopped
4 cups of shredded Italian cheese
1 pound of Portobello mushrooms, quartered
1 medium-sized green capsicum, chopped
1 medium-sized red capsicum, chopped
2 garlic cloves, minced
12 Oz of baby spinach
8 slices of Italian bread, 1-inch thick
1 cup of milk
½ teaspoon of salt
½ teaspoon of pepper
1 teaspoon of Italian seasoning
¼ teaspoon of ground nutmeg

Preparation

Heat a skillet over medium heat; add the sausage, peppers, onion, mushrooms and garlic. Cook until the pink color disappears. Drain the excess liquid and set aside. Sauté the spinach in a large oiled skillet only until it wilts. Place them into a baking sheet. Broil for about 3 minutes until lightly brown and transfer into a baking dish. Into a bowl, whisk the eggs, nutmeg, Italian seasoning, salt and pepper. Add a layer of the sausage mixture and spinach over the bread slices, top with the egg mixture, sprinkle with cheese, cover and refrigerate overnight. Allow to rest for 30 minutes after removing from the fridge. Bake for about 60 minutes in a preheated oven at a temperature of 350 F and let it cool before serving.

Italian Roasted Potatoes

Preparation time: 15 minutes

Cooking time: 50 minutes

Nutrition facts (per serving): 190 Cal (fats 0g, proteins 5g, fibers 6g)

Ingredients (2 servings)

2 medium-sized potatoes

¼ teaspoon of smoked paprika

½ teaspoon of chili powder

½ teaspoon of dried dill

½ teaspoon of minced garlic

2 tablespoons of chopped parsley

½ red bell pepper, sliced

½ of a medium-sized onion, sliced

Preparation

Cut the potatoes into large pieces and boil them until soft. Sauté the onions, add the bell peppers and cook until soft. Drain the potatoes, place them on a prepared baking sheet and add the onion mixture, garlic, onion powder and herbs. Bake in a preheated oven at 375 F for 45 minutes until crispy and golden.

Baked Eggs and Veggies

Preparation time: 15 minutes

Cooking time: 50 minutes

Nutrition facts (per serving): 149 Cal (fats 6.7g, proteins 10.8g, fibers 3g)

Ingredients (2 servings)

4 eggs

$1/4$ cup of grated parmesan cheese

1 pound of plum tomatoes, cut into 1-inch chunks

2 garlic cloves, minced

1 red bell pepper, cut into small pieces

$1/4$ teaspoon of black pepper

½ teaspoon of salt

1 zucchini, quartered lengthwise and cut into chunks

1 onion, sliced

½ teaspoon of dried basil

Preparation

Add the tomatoes, garlic, bell pepper, onion, zucchini, basil and pepper in oil sprayed pan and toss. Roast in a preheated oven at 400 F for 35 minutes, until brown. Spray the custard cups with a nonstick spray, divide the vegetables between them, make a well at the center of the vegetables and break the eggs in. Sprinkle with parmesan and bake for 25 minutes until the eggs are set.

Oven-Baked Eggs and Asparagus

Preparation time: 15 minutes

Cooking time: 40 minutes

Nutrition facts (per serving): 130 Cal (fats 9g, Proteins 10g, fibers 1g)

Ingredients (2 servings)

1 bundle of asparagus, trimmed and cut into chunks

10 eggs, beaten

2 teaspoons of olive oil

½ of a large onion, cut into thin crescents

Salt and pepper

¾ cup of grated parmesan cheese

Preparation

Heat the oil in a skillet, sauté the onions, add the asparagus and cook until crispy. Season with pepper and salt and set aside. Grease the cups and divide the eggs and vegetables between them. Top with cheese and bake in a preheated oven at 380 F for about 27-31 minutes, or until the top browns.

Main Dishes

Roasted Veggies Antipasto Plate

Preparation time: 20 minutes

Cooking time: 40 minutes

Nutrition facts (per serving): 117 Cal (fats 8.2g, proteins 662g, fibers 3.8g)

Ingredients (6 servings)

12 medium-sized sprouts, trimmed and halved

4 tablespoons of olive oil

1 large fennel bulb, cut into ¼-inch wedges

8 Oz (12 small) of carrots

1 large beet, sliced

1 garlic clove, sliced into small rounds

1 teaspoon of salt

1 garlic clove, minced

1 anchovy fillet

1 teaspoon of chopped capers

2 tablespoons of lemon juice

Preparation

Toss the sprouts with 1 teaspoon of olive oil and spread them on one half of a large baking sheet. Toss the fennel with 1 teaspoon of olive oil and spread them on the other half. Toss the beet and carrots with olive oil and place each on each half of the second baking sheet. Sprinkle both sheets with vegetables and salt, then roast for 27-32 minutes. Mash the garlic and ½ a teaspoon of salt to form a paste, add capers, lemon juice and 2 tablespoons of olive oil and whisk. Drizzle the mixture over the veggies and serve.

Italian Arancini Balls

Preparation time: 40 minutes
Cooking time: 70 minutes
Nutrition facts (per serving): 266 Cal (fats 11g, proteins 11g, fibers 1g)

Ingredients (6 servings)

2 tablespoons of olive oil

½ Oz of unsalted butter

1 onion, finely chopped

12 Oz of risotto rice

2/3 cup of white wine

5 Oz of bread crumbs

1 garlic clove, minced

3 eggs

5 Oz of parmesan cheese, grated

Grated lemon zest

6 Oz of mozzarella ball, chopped into 18 pieces

5 Oz of flour

Vegetable oil

Preparation

Sauté the garlic and onion in butter until translucent. Add some salt and stir in the rice, pour the wine in and bring to boil. Simmer until the rice cooks through, stir in the grated lemon zest and parmesan. Spread the risotto into a tray, allow it to cool and then shape into 18 balls. Flatten the risotto balls with your palm and add mozzarella in the center, roll into balls once more. Dip the balls in flour, then in the beaten eggs, coat with breadcrumbs and set aside. Deep fry the balls until golden brown. Serve with tomato sauce for dipping.

Italian Tuna Balls

Preparation time: 10 minutes

Cooking time: 15 minutes

Nutrition facts (per serving): 594 Cal (fats 12g, proteins 35g, fibers 4g)

Ingredients (4 servings)

11 Oz of tuna

A handful of pine nuts

Grated lemon zest

1 pound of pasta sauce

14 Oz of spaghetti

1 egg, beaten

2 Oz of breadcrumbs

A handful of parsley, chopped

Preparation

Into a bowl, mix the egg, parsley, flaked tuna, pine nuts, lemon zest and breadcrumbs, season and roll into walnut-sized balls. Fry the balls in oil until golden brown. Boil the spaghetti in salted water. Heat the tomato sauce, toss the balls and pasta in and serve.

Spinach Ricotta Aubergine Rolls

Preparation time: 15 minutes
Cooking time: 45 minutes
Nutrition facts (per serving): 376 Cal (fats 23g, Proteins 20 g, fibers 10g)

Ingredients (4 servings)

4 tablespoons of parmesan cheese

4 tablespoons of breadcrumbs

2 eggplants, halved lengthwise

2 tablespoons of olive oil

12 Oz of tomato sauce

8-oz tub of ricotta

17 Oz of spinach

Some grated nutmeg

Preparation

Brush the eggplant slices with some olive oil and bake at 400 F for about 22-26 minutes. Pour the spinach in boiling water. Cool, squeeze the excess water out and mix with the ricotta, seasonings and nutmeg. Place a spoonful of the cheesy spinach at the center of each eggplant slice and fold it over. Add some tomato sauce on the slices, sprinkle with breadcrumbs and cheese and bake for about 22-25 minutes, or until golden brown.

Italian Lamb Tagliata with Tomatoes and Watercress

Preparation time: 10 minutes
Cooking time: 5 minutes
Nutrition facts (per serving): 334 Cal (fats 22g, Proteins 28g, fibers 2g)

Ingredients (4 servings)
2 tablespoons of olive oil
1 pound of lamb steak
A handful of rosemary needles, chopped
8 Oz (250g) of British plum tomato
1 tablespoon of redcurrant jelly
2 tablespoons of capers, drained and rinsed
2 tablespoons of balsamic vinegar
3 Oz (100g) of feta cheese
3 Oz (100g) of British watercress
Salt and black pepper
Crusty bread to serve

Preparation
Add 1 tablespoon of olive oil to the rosemary and marinate the lamb in it for 40 minutes. Wipe most of the rosemary out and season the steak with salt and black pepper. Sear the meat and tomatoes for about 3 minutes, or until golden and set aside. Whisk the vinegar, redcurrant jelly and oil into a pan and warm until the dressing is made. Slice the lamb and spread the watercress and tomatoes on it, followed by cheese. Spoon over the dressing and serve with crusty bread.

Vegan Casarecce with Tomato Sauce

Preparation time: 5 minutes

Cooking time: 10 minutes

Nutrition facts (per serving): 596 Cal (fats 24.3g, proteins 14g, fibers 6.9g)

Ingredients (2 servings)

17 Oz (500g) of halved cherry tomatoes

3 finely chopped spring onions

4 tablespoons of olive oil

3 tablespoons of red wine vinegar

7 Oz (200g) of casarecce (or other short twisted pasta)

5 dashes of Tabasco

Salt and pepper

Basil leaves

Preparation

In a bowl, mix the onions, cherry tomatoes, olive oil, vinegar and Tabasco and season them with salt and pepper. Add the casarecce into salted boiling water and cook until ready. Add 2 tablespoons of water to the sauce and toss the pasta in. Serve garnished with the basil.

Fried Gnocchi with Broad Beans, Sage and Ricotta

Preparation time: 5 minutes

Cooking time: 15 minutes

Nutrition facts (per serving): 252 Cal (fats 12g, Proteins 12.2g, fibers 3.7g)

Ingredients (6 servings)

18-oz (250g) tub of ricotta

2 tablespoons of olive oil

1 garlic clove, minced

14 Oz (400g) of gnocchi

6 slices of Parma ham

Lemon zest

Some butter

A handful of sage leaves

Preparation

Mix the ricotta, zest and seasoning in a bowl. Spread the mixture on the bottom of a serving dish and set aside. Grill the Parma ham until crispy. Add the gnocchi into salted boiling water and scoop out immediately after floating. Fry the garlic, fry the gnocchi in batches and cook until crispy. Fry the sage with butter and spoon it on warm gnocchi.

Italian Chipolata Sausage and Roasted Veggies

Preparation time: 10 minutes
Cooking time: 20 minutes
Nutrition facts (per serving): 475 Cal (fats 37.5g, proteins 14.5g, fibers 6.2g)

Ingredients (4 servings)

14 Oz (400g) of chipolata sausages

4 tablespoons of fresh pesto

7 Oz (200g) of cherry tomatoes

2 garlic cloves, minced

1 red onion, cut into wedges

2 zucchinis, cut into half-moon shapes

1 red capsicum, chopped

Basil leaves

Olive oil

Preparation

Toss the chipolata sausages in a little olive oil and bake at 400 F for about 11-13 minutes, or until they are tender. Toss the tomatoes, zucchini, onion and capsicum with olive oil and add them to the baked chipolatas. Bake for another 45 minutes, or until golden. Mix the pesto with some olive oil and a splash of water. Drizzle the mixture over the baked veggies, garnish with basil.

Italian Chicken with Agrodolce Sauce

Preparation time: 5 minutes

Cooking time: 15 minutes

Nutrition facts (per serving): 262 Cal (fats 7.6g, proteins 35.8g, fibers 2.3g)

Ingredients (2 servings)

2 skinless chicken breasts, sliced horizontally into 4 pieces

1 tablespoon of flour

½ teaspoon of sugar

3 Oz (100g) of halved cherry tomatoes

1 red onion, thinly sliced

3 celery stalks, thinly sliced

1 tablespoon of red wine vinegar

A handful of parsley, chopped

Olive oil

Preparation

Cover the chicken pieces with baking paper and flatten them using a rolling pin. Dust with flour and shake the excess off. Brown both sides of the chicken in 1 tablespoon of olive oil. In a nonstick pan, cook the onion and celery for about 4 minutes, season and stir in the tomatoes. Cook until they begin to break up. Stir the chicken in and add the parsley to taste.

Baked Passata Meatballs

Preparation time: 35 minutes

Cooking time: 65 minutes

Nutrition facts (per serving): 617 Cal (fats 39.2, proteins 31.9g, fibers 4g)

Ingredients (6 servings)

3 onions, diced

5 garlic cloves, minced

3 bay leaves

14 Oz (400g) of tomatoes, chopped

2 ½ cups (600ml) of passata

1 egg

3 ½ Oz (100g) of mascarpone

2 tablespoons of tomato puree

1 cup (125g) of breadcrumbs

18 Oz (500g) of minced beef

Olive oil

1 tablespoon of red wine vinegar

1 tablespoon of brown sugar

1 tablespoon of fennel seeds

1 tablespoon of dried oregano

8 Oz (250g) of mozzarella

Preparation

Fry the onions and garlic with 2 tablespoons of olive oil until soft. Scoop half of it into a bowl. Add the passata, tomato puree, sugar, tomatoes and vinegar into a pan, simmer until it thickens and then add the seasoning. Add the reserved onions, eggs, beef, breadcrumbs, fennel seeds, oregano and seasoning and mix well. Shape the mixture into balls and fry in oil until they are done. Cool at room temperature. Mix half of the mozzarella, mascarpone and some salt. Add the balls into the tomato sauce in a dish, blob the mozzarella mixture over and freeze. Cover the dish and bake until the top of the cheese is golden. Allow to cool. Drizzle with oil and sprinkle with some oregano.

Italian Fritto Misto

Preparation time: 20 minutes
Cooking time: 15 minutes
Nutrition facts (per serving): 270 Cal (fats 7g, proteins 1g, fibers 44g)

Ingredients (6 servings)
8 cups of vegetable oil
1 cup of flour
1 cup of cornstarch
4 Oz of squid
4 Oz of deveined shrimps, halved
2 cups of chilled club soda
1 teaspoon of baking powder
¼ of a small squash, thinly sliced
½ of a fennel bulb, thinly sliced
1 leek, halved lengthwise
2 Oz of shiitake mushrooms
1 lemon, cut into wedges
¼ cup of sage leaves
½ cup of parsley leaves
Salt

Preparation
Whisk the flour, baking powder, ½ a teaspoon of salt and cornstarch into a bowl. Stir in the club soda. Dip the seafood, vegetables, lemon and herbs into the batter as you fry them. Turn them occasionally and cook until crispy and golden. Transfer them on a plate lined with a paper towel, season with salt and serve warm.

Italian Instant Pot Beef Sandwiches

Preparation time: 15 minutes

Cooking time: 95 minutes

Nutrition facts (per serving): 614 Cal (fats 25.1g, proteins 53.4g, fibers 3.9g)

Ingredients (6 servings)

3 pounds of beef chuck roast, cut into chunks

1 teaspoon of paprika

2 teaspoons of dried oregano

1 teaspoon of dried basil

1 teaspoon of onion powder

3 garlic cloves, minced

½ teaspoon of garlic powder

½ of a medium-sized onion, diced

1 teaspoon of salt

3 cups of beef broth

½ teaspoon of black pepper

½ teaspoon of red pepper flakes

6 sandwich rolls

Mix of veggies (for example DeLallo giardiniera)

Sliced provolone

Preparation

Add all the ingredients in an instant pot and cook on high pressure for 55 minutes. Shred the beef and save the juices in the pot for later use. Layer each side of the bun with a slice of provolone and broil until melty. Top it with beef and veggies. Use the broth as your dip.

Beef Braciole

Preparation time: 30 minutes
Cooking time: 120 minutes
Nutrition facts (per serving): 357 Cal (fats 16g, Proteins 29g, fibers 1g)

Ingredients (2 servings)

1 cup of shredded parmesan

2 tablespoons of seasoned breadcrumbs

6 slices of boneless top round

12 garlic cloves, 4 minced, 8 sliced

½ cup of finely chopped parsley

1 can of crushed tomatoes

2 tablespoons of olive oil

2 teaspoons of Italian seasoning

2 cups of beef broth

2 cups of dry red wine

12 thin slices of prosciutto

Salt and black pepper

2 tablespoons of all-purpose flour

Preparation

Halve the top-round slices lengthwise, place the beef between two pieces of plastic wrap and pound to ¼-inch thickness. Mix the cheese, salt, garlic, breadcrumbs and pepper to make the filling. Place the prosciutto over the beef, sprinkle it with the filling evenly and roll. Secure the rolls with toothpicks, fry in olive oil until they brown. Place the rolls on a plate and set aside. Boil the slices of garlic in wine, add the seasoning, tomatoes and broth, place the beef rolls and simmer until thickened, as you stir occasionally. Season with salt and pepper and serve over pasta.

Porcini Beef Stew

Preparation time: 40 minutes

Cooking time: 150 minutes

Nutrition facts (per serving): 692 Cal (fats 34g, Proteins 64g, fibers 4g)

Ingredients (8 servings)

4 ½ pounds of sliced beefsteak

¼ cup (57g) of unsalted butter

1.4 Oz (40g) of porcini pieces

7-oz (200g) pack of pancetta

3 tablespoons of sunflower oil

1 tablespoon of light brown sugar

2 large onions, sliced

6 fresh springs of thyme leaves

2 tablespoons of Worcestershire sauce

7-oz (200g) pack of chestnuts, peeled, cooked

4 garlic cloves, minced

¾ cup of flour

4 cups of beef stock

$1/3$ cup (90ml) of Italian red wine

$1/3$ cup of ruby port

Preparation

Soak the porcini pieces in boiling water for 30 minutes, strain and set aside. Fry the pancetta with 2 tablespoons of oil until lightly golden and set aside. Brown the beef with some oil and set aside. Fry the onions with 1 tablespoon of oil and half of the butter. Stir some salt and sugar in and fry until the onions brown. Add the garlic to the onions, fry for 5 minutes, then stir in the porcini, followed by the porcini liquid and simmer until the amount of the fluid reduces. Stir in the flour, add the stock and red wine and bring to a boil. Then add the pancetta, beef, Worcestershire sauce and thyme leaves and bring to a boil. Cover with foil and bake the mixture for about 120-130 minutes. Add some chestnuts, adjust the seasoning and bake for 40 minutes more. Mash the remaining butter and flour to make a paste. Stir the paste into the stew and simmer until it thickens. Allow the casserole to cool and serve.

Beef with Borlotti Beans

Preparation time: 25 minutes

Cooking time: 120 minutes

Nutrition facts (per serving): 682 Cal (fats 31g, Proteins 63g, fibers 6g)

Ingredients (6 servings)

3 1/3 pounds (1.5kg) of minced beef brisket

2 teaspoons of olive oil

3 Oz (100g) of pancetta

14-oz can of thick tomato paste

14-oz can of borlotti beans, drained and rinsed

½ cup of chopped parsley

1 garlic clove, minced

2 celery sticks, chopped

1 brown onion, coarsely chopped

1 carrot, coarsely chopped

2 garlic cloves, minced

½ cup of red wine

2 fresh rosemary springs

2 dried bay leaves

Grated lemon zest

Preparation

Season and brown the beef, then set it aside. On the medium-high setting of the pressure cooker, cook the pancetta, garlic, carrot, onion and celery until soft. Add the tomato paste, wine, rosemary and bay leaves and simmer for 6 minutes. Add the beef in to nestle on the vegetables, cook on high pressure for 42-44 minutes, set aside and warm the beans. Make the gremolata by mixing 1 minced garlic clove with parsley and lemon. Add the beans into the beef and sprinkle with gremolata.

Italian Roast Beef

Preparation time: 15 minutes

Cooking time: 8 hours

Nutrition facts (per serving): 840 Cal (fats 51g, Proteins 69g, Fibers 6g)

Ingredients (6 servings)

3-pound beef chuck roast

1 ½ teaspoons of salt

2 cups of celery, cut diagonally

3 cups of carrots, peeled, cut diagonally

2 cups of coarsely chopped white onion

¼ cup of Land O'Lakes butter

1 teaspoon of pepper

6-oz can of garlic, basil, oregano and tomato paste

15-oz can of diced tomatoes

Preparation

Pat dry the beef and sprinkle it with salt and pepper. Cook it in melted butter until it browns and set it aside. Combine the onions, celery, carrots, tomatoes and tomato paste. Place the mixture at the bottom of a slow cooker, add the beef, cover and cook on high setting for 7 hours or a bit more.

Instant Italian Pot Roast

Preparation time: 5 minutes

Cooking time: 45 minutes

Nutrition facts (per serving): 457 Cal (fats 19g, Proteins 36g, fibers 5g)

Ingredients (8 servings)

3 pounds of beef chuck roast

3 pounds of small red potatoes, quartered

3 cups of carrots, quartered

¼ cup of water

15-oz can of tomato sauce

1 package of thick and zesty spaghetti sauce mix

Preparation

Add the potatoes at the bottom of the instant pot, layer the carrots on top and add water. Place the beef chunk on the carrot layer. Mix the tomato sauce and spaghetti sauce mix and pour it over the roast. Set the cooker on a meat setting and cook for about 45 minutes.

Italian Beef with Vegetables

Preparation time: 10 minutes
Cooking time: 30 minutes
Nutrition facts (per serving): 315 Cal (fats 18g, Proteins 19g, Fibers 5g)

Ingredients (6 servings)

1 pound of ground beef
2 garlic cloves, minced
2 cups of chopped green cabbage
½ teaspoon of black pepper
½ teaspoon of salt
½ cup of diced yellow onion
2 cups of thinly sliced carrots
3 stalks of celery
¼ teaspoon of dried thyme
½ teaspoon of dried basil
1 teaspoon of dried oregano
8-oz can of diced tomatoes
14-oz can of crushed tomatoes
7-oz can of tomato sauce
3 cups of water

Preparation

Cook and crumble the beef along with the onions and garlic for 7-9 minutes, or until it browns. Add the water, carrots and celery. Increase the heat to high and add the oregano, basil, tomato sauce, crushed tomatoes, diced tomatoes, thyme, salt and pepper. Cover, bring to a boil and simmer until the carrots are tender. Stir in the cabbage and cook until they wilt. Top with cheese and serve.

Italian Beef Hoagies

Preparation time: 10 minutes

Cooking time: 4 hours

Nutrition facts (per serving): 621 Cal (fats 25g, Proteins 55g, fibers 3g)

Ingredients (6 servings)

16 Oz of pepperoncini, without stems

1 tablespoon of minced garlic

1 tablespoon of Italian seasoning

2 pounds of roast beef

6 large sub rolls

½ teaspoon of salt

½ cup of beef stock

12 slices of Swiss cheese

1/2 teaspoon of ground black pepper

Preparation

Add all the ingredients into a slow cooker and set it at 4 hours on high. Shred the beef and return it into the cooker to soak up the juices. Toast the sub rolls, sandwich the meat in-between, add the cheese, top with pepperoncini and serve.

Lasagna Rolls with Baked Chicken

Preparation time: 10 minutes

Cooking time: 45 minutes

Nutrition facts (per serving): 370.1 Cal (fats 15.7g, proteins 31.2g, fibers 1.6g)

Ingredients (6 servings)

½ cup of parmesan cheese

1 egg

2 cups of ricotta cheese

1 ¼ cups of shredded mozzarella cheese

1 teaspoon of garlic powder

1 ½ cups of tomato sauce

8 cooked lasagna noodles

2 cups of shredded cooked chicken

½ teaspoon of black pepper

½ teaspoon of salt

¼ cup of chopped parsley

Preparation

Reserve ¼ cup of mozzarella cheese. Mix the other cheeses, egg, garlic, parsley, salt and black pepper. Place the noodles on a plastic wrap, top each one with a layer of ricotta mixture and chicken. Roll each noodle, fill the baking dish with ½ cup of tomato sauce and sprinkle with mozzarella. Bake for about 22-24 minutes.

Italian Chicken Marsala

Preparation time: 10 minutes
Cooking time: 20 minutes
Nutrition facts (per serving): 447.7 Cal (fats 26.6g, proteins 28.8g, fibers 1.6g)

Ingredients (4 servings)

4 pounded chicken breasts

¼ cup of flour

1 cup of sliced mushrooms

½ teaspoon of dried oregano

½ teaspoon of salt

¼ teaspoon of ground black pepper

4 tablespoons of butter

½ cup of cooking sherry

½ cup of Marsala wine

4 tablespoons of olive oil

Preparation

Mix the oregano, flour, salt and pepper. Coat the chicken pieces with the mixture. In a skillet, brown the chicken in butter, turn and add the mushrooms. Pour the sherry and wine in, cover and simmer for about 12-13 minutes, or until the juices are absorbed.

Italian Parmesan Garlic Chicken

Preparation time: 5 minutes

Cooking time: 25 minutes

Nutrition facts (per serving): 216 Cal (fats 7g, proteins 36g, fibers 0g)

Ingredients (6 servings)

6 boneless chicken breasts

½ cup of grated parmesan cheese

2 packs of Good Seasons dressing mix

1 teaspoon of ground garlic

Preparation

Preheat the oven to 400 F. Mix the garlic, cheese and dressing and dredge the chicken in the mixture. Bake the chicken for about 26-28 minutes, or until cooked through.

Italian Chicken Piccata

Preparation time: 15 minutes
Cooking time: 35 minutes
Nutrition facts (per serving): 4251 Cal (fats 8g, proteins 37g, fibers 1g)

Ingredients (4 servings)

1 1/3 pounds of boneless skinless chicken breast

3 tablespoons of water

2 tablespoons of parmesan cheese

2 roman tomatoes

½ cup of mozzarella cheese

2 tablespoons of balsamic vinegar

2 garlic cloves

1 tablespoon of lemon juice

1/8 teaspoon of salt

1/8 teaspoon of black pepper

1 cup of fresh basil

2 teaspoons of olive oil

2 tablespoons of almonds

Preparation

Preheat the oven to 400 F. Into a blender or food processor, pulse the basil, parmesan, pepper, water, olive oil, lemon juice, almonds, garlic and salt, to make pesto. Spray a baking dish with cooking spray and place the chicken in. Season with salt and pepper. Spread the pesto on the chicken, top with cheese and tomatoes and bake for about 34-37 minutes, or until cooked through. Drizzle with balsamic vinegar before serving.

Milk Cooked Pork Loin

Preparation time: 15 minutes

Cooking time: 100 minutes

Nutrition facts (per serving): 1565 Cal (fats 210g, proteins 236g, fibers 0.4g)

Ingredients

1 ½ pounds of boneless pork loin

3 garlic cloves, minced

¼ teaspoon of black pepper

2 tablespoons of white wine vinegar

4 tablespoons of olive oil

1 tablespoon of rosemary

1 ½ cups of milk

Preparation

Rub the pork with oil, garlic, pepper and rosemary and marinate for about 130 minutes. Brown the pork with 2 tablespoons of oil, add the milk and vinegar, cover and turn twice. Cook until tender. Put the meat on a board and cover with foil, thicken the liquid in the pan and season it with salt and pepper. Slice the pork, pour the thick sauce over it and serve.

Italian Meatloaf

Preparation time: 20 minutes
Cooking time: 60 minutes

Ingredients

2 pounds of ground beef
2 eggs
1 carrot, grated
1/2 onion, chopped
2 garlic cloves, minced
1/2 cup of chopped fresh parsley
1/2 cup of ketchup
1 1/2 cups of fresh breadcrumbs
1 cup of tomato sauce
1 teaspoon of white sugar

Preparation

Preheat the oven to 380 F. Sauté the onions and carrots in a medium saucepan over a medium high heat for 2-3 minutes, or until the onions are transparent. Add the garlic and sauté for another 3 minutes. Remove from the heat and let it cool. In a large bowl, combine the beef, parsley, ketchup, 1/2 cup of tomato sauce, bread and eggs and mix well. Add the carrot/onion mixture and continue mixing, but do not over mix, as this will make the meatloaf dry. Transfer the mixture to a 9x13-inch baking dish and form into a loaf. Bake in the oven for 42-47 minutes. While the loaf is baking, heat the remaining tomato sauce and sugar in a medium saucepan over medium low heat. Pour over the loaf when done.

Easy Bologna Chicken

Preparation time: 20 minutes

Cooking time: 40 minutes

Ingredients

8 chicken legs, halved

1 tablespoon of crushed red pepper flakes

4 garlic cloves

1/2 cup of water

1 tablespoon of vegetable oil

Salt to taste

Preparation

In a large skillet, brown the chicken pieces in oil. Cook for 14-16 minutes on a medium heat. Crush the garlic cloves and squeeze them over the chicken. Cover the skillet and cook on low heat for 12 minutes on each side. Remove the cover, sprinkle with the red pepper flakes and salt to taste, add water and simmer over low heat until the water evaporates and the chicken pieces are sticky.

Italian Balsamic Roasted Pork Loin

Preparation time: 5 minutes
Cooking time: 65 minutes
Nutrition facts (per serving): 299 Cal (fats 23.4g, proteins 18.3g, fibers 0.1g)

Ingredients (4 servings)

½ cup of olive oil
½ cup of balsamic vinegar
2 tablespoons of Italian seasoning
2 pounds of boneless pork loin roast

Preparation

Make a marinade from the vinegar and oil. Place the steak in a sealable plastic bag and pour the marinade on the pork. Squeeze the air out, seal the bag and marinate for 110-130 minutes or more. Bake the pork along with the marinade at 350 F for 55-70 minutes, or until the internal temperature of the pork reaches 145 F. Wait for 10-15 minutes before serving.

Spicy Pork Cutlets

Preparation time: 15 minutes

Cooking time: 20 minutes

Nutrition facts (per serving): 260 Cal (fats 18.7g, proteins 16.1g, fibers 0.8g)

Ingredients (2 servings)

4 pounded boneless pork chops

$1/3$ cup of chicken broth

¼ cup of olive oil

4 garlic cloves, thinly sliced

1 tomato, diced

¼ cup of white wine

¼ cup of red pepper flakes

Salt and pepper

Preparation

Heat 2 tablespoons of oil and add the pork chops in, season with salt and pepper. Sear both sides and set aside. Into a bowl, mix the pepper flakes, tomato, wine, parsley and chicken broth. Heat the remaining oil and sauté the garlic, add the broth mixture and cook stirring until it thickens. Stir in the pork and cook for another 6-7 minutes. Serve together with the broth mixture.

Breaded Pork Chops

Preparation time: 25 minutes

Cooking time: 35 minutes

Nutrition facts (per serving): 440 Cal (fats 20.3g, proteins 30g, fibers 0.8g)

Ingredients (4 servings)

4 pork chops

2 tablespoons of dried parsley

3 eggs, lightly beaten

4 garlic cloves, chopped

2 tablespoons of olive oil

½ cup of grated parmesan cheese

1 ½ cups of Italian seasoned bread crumbs

3 tablespoons of milk

Preparation

Preheat the oven to 325 F. Mix the cheese, breadcrumbs and parsley. Cook the garlic in oil until it has lightly browned, remove from oil and set aside. Dip the meat chops into the egg mixture, then coat them with the breadcrumbs evenly. Toast them in the oil in a skillet. Bake the pork chops in the skillet for 24-28 minutes and serve with the garlic.

Italian Braised Pork Ragu

Preparation time: 10 minutes
Cooking time: 60 minutes
Nutrition facts (per serving): 263 Cal (fats 13,7g, proteins 19g, fibers 2.3g)

Ingredients (6 servings)

2 pounds of pork roast, cut into cubes

1 teaspoon of crumbled dried rosemary

28-oz can of diced tomatoes

1 cup of chicken broth

1 onion, diced

1 teaspoon of dried thyme

1 carrot, peeled and diced

½ cup of dry red wine

2 garlic cloves, minced

2 tablespoon of olive oil

½ teaspoon of salt

1 teaspoon of ground black pepper

Preparation

Season the meat with rosemary, thyme, salt and pepper and sear the seasoned pork in hot oil until it browns on both sides. Stir the carrots and onions in and cook until the onions become tender. Pour in the wine, stir the tomatoes and stock in. Bring to a boil and simmer for about 27-32 minutes until the sauce thickens.

Italian Pork Tenderloin

Preparation time: 20 minutes
Cooking time: 30 minutes
Nutrition facts (per serving): 532 Cal (fats 17.1g, proteins 83.3g, fibers 1.3g)

Ingredients (4 servings)

2 garlic cloves, minced

1 red capsicum, halved and deseeded

15 black olives, pitted oil-cured

3 ½ pounds of pork tenderloin

1 teaspoon of mustard

1 onion, thinly sliced

4 fresh mushrooms

1 tablespoon of brown sauce

Salt and pepper

Preparation

Slice the pork lengthwise, spread the chopped olives and garlic on the roast and sprinkle with salt and pepper. Tie the loin at an interval of 1 inch, shape into a roll. Marinate and keep refrigerated for at least 14 hours or more. Place the sliced capsicum on a foil, followed by the pork on top. Cover the surface with the browning sauce and then place the onions and mushrooms on top. Seal the foil and make a small tent on top. Grill for 22 minutes, or until the internal temperature reaches 150 F. Let the pork rest for about 12 minutes before slicing. Place the red pepper on the roasting pan, place the tenderloin on top and add the browning sauce, followed by the mushrooms and onions. Cover and bake at 375 F for about 31-34 minutes. Cool before serving.

Shiitake Mushroom and Pork Ragu

Preparation time: 20 minutes
Cooking time: 4 hours
Nutrition facts (per serving): 299 Cal (fats 19.6g, proteins 20.2g, fibers 2.4g)

Ingredients (8 servings)

1 cup of chicken broth

4 garlic cloves, minced

2 tablespoons of coconut oil

8 Oz of shiitake mushrooms, sliced

3 pounds of pork roast, cut into chunks

28-oz can of diced tomatoes

2 bay leaves

1 tablespoon of Italian seasoning

6-oz can of tomato paste

Salt and pepper

Preparation

Season the meat with salt and pepper. Cook the pork in hot oil until it browns on both sides. Add the garlic, bay leaves, chicken broth and seasoning in and cook for a while. Add the tomato and tomato paste in, reduce the heat and cook for 150 minutes. Remove from the heat and shred the pork into the sauce. Add the mushrooms, cover and simmer for 55-65 minutes. Remove the bay leaves and serve.

Italian Pepper Onion Sausage

Preparation time: 15 minutes

Cooking time: 25 minutes

Nutrition facts (per serving): 461 Cal (fats 39.4g, proteins 17.1g, fibers 1.6g)

Ingredients (6 servings)

6 links of Italian sausage (4 Oz)

1 yellow onion, sliced

½ red onion, sliced

2 tablespoons of butter

4 garlic cloves, minced

1 red capsicum, sliced

1 green capsicum, sliced

1 teaspoon of dried basil

1 teaspoon of dried oregano

¼ cup of white wine

Preparation

Brown the sausage in oil, slice and set aside. Cook the garlic and onions in melted butter. Add the peppers and then season with basil and oregano. Stir the white wine in and cook until the vegetables are tender. Stir in the sausage, simmer for 14-17 minutes and serve.

Italian Meatballs

Preparation time: 30 minutes

Cooking time: 20 minutes

Nutrition facts (per serving): 613 Cal (fats 53.2g, proteins 26.6, fibers 0.3g)

Ingredients (8 servings)

1 pound of beef

½ pound of pork

½ pound of veal

2 garlic cloves, minced

2 eggs

1 cup of grated Romano cheese

2 cups of crumbled stale Italian bread

1 ½ tablespoons of chopped parsley

1 ½ cups of warm water

1 cup of olive oil

Salt and black pepper

Preparation

Combine the veal, pork and beef in a bowl. Add the garlic, eggs, cheese, parsley, salt and pepper. Add the breadcrumbs, moisten with water slowly and shape the mixture into balls. Fry the mixture balls in oil until they are slightly crispy and brown. Serve with sauce to taste.

Roasted Pork Loins

Preparation time: 20 minutes
Cooking time: 60 minutes
Nutrition facts (per serving): 238 Cal (fats 16.2g, proteins 18.4g, fibers 0.2g)

Ingredients (8 servings)

2 pounds of pork loin roast steak

½ cup of white wine

1 teaspoon of dried rosemary

½ cup of olive oil

3 garlic cloves, minced

Salt and pepper

Preparation

Into a food processor, pulse the garlic, rosemary, salt and pepper to make a paste. Pierce the meat in several places with a knife and place the paste on the pierced areas. Rub with olive oil and the remaining paste and roast at 350 F for 55-65 minutes. Place the roast into a platter, heat the wine and stir to loosen the bits of food. Serve with the pan juices.

Pork Marsala

Preparation time: 10 minutes
Cooking time: 20 minutes
Nutrition facts (per serving): 455 Cal (fats 27.6g, proteins 17.6g, fibers 0.8g)

Ingredients (4 servings)

1 pound of pork loin chops, pounded

¼ cup of olive oil

2 cups of fresh mushrooms, sliced

3 tablespoons of butter

¼ teaspoon of salt

½ teaspoon of dried oregano

1 teaspoon of garlic powder

$^1/_3$ cup of flour

1 cup of marsala wine

¼ teaspoon of garlic salt

1 teaspoon of minced garlic

Preparation

Into a bowl, mix the garlic, garlic powder, flour, oregano and salt. Add the pork and toss until it coats well. Brown the meat in butter and olive oil, add the minced garlic and mushrooms and cook stirring. Stir the wine in, cover and simmer for the sauce to thicken.

Stuffed Banana Peppers

Preparation time: 30 minutes
Cooking time: 90 minutes
Nutrition facts (per serving): 593 Cal (fats 42.5g, proteins 25.1g, fibers 5.2g)

Ingredients (4 servings)

8 banana peppers, seedless
½ cup of chopped onion
½ cup of chopped celery
2 tablespoons of butter
28-oz can of crushed tomatoes
8-oz can of tomato sauce
2 garlic cloves, minced
1 teaspoon of dried oregano
½ teaspoon of ground black pepper
1 egg
1 teaspoon of dried basil
1 teaspoon of Worcestershire sauce
1 ½ cups of breadcrumbs
1 pound of hot Italian sauce
1 pound of mild Italian sauce
½ cup of grated parmesan cheese
Salt

Preparation

Take the peppers, chop the tops off and remove the seeds. Add the peppers in boiling salty water, simmer for 6-7 minutes and set aside. Sauté the chopped pepper tops, onions and celery until tender. Stir in the garlic, crushed tomatoes and tomato sauce. Season with oregano, 1 ½ teaspoons of salt and ¼ teaspoon of pepper. Cover and simmer for 11-12 minutes. Mix with the parmesan, eggs,

1 teaspoon of salt, Worcestershire sauce and ¼ teaspoon of pepper. In another bowl, mix the sausages, 1 cup of tomato sauce mixture and bread crumbs. Fill each pepper with the meat mixture and place in a casserole dish; pour the remaining sauce over the peppers and bake at 350F for 70-75 minutes.

Italian Slow Cooker Pork Cacciatore

Preparation time: 15 minutes
Cooking time: 8 hours
Nutrition facts (per serving): 614 Cal (fats 31g, proteins 34.5g, fibers 8.4g)

Ingredients (4 servings)

28-oz can of diced tomatoes

1 onion, sliced

8-oz pack of sliced mushroom

4 slices of mozzarella cheese

4 boneless pork chops

28 Oz of pasta sauce

2 tablespoons of olive oil

1 green capsicum, seeded, sliced into strips

2 garlic cloves, minced

1 teaspoon of Italian seasoning

½ cup of dry white wine

½ teaspoon of dried basil

Preparation

Brown the pork chops and transfer them into a slow cooker. Cook the onions in a pan until they brown, stir the capsicum and mushrooms in and cook until tender. Add the pasta sauce, wine and tomatoes. Season with Italian seasoning, garlic and basil, then pour over the meat chops and slow cook for 8 hours on a low setting. Place the slices of cheese over the pork chops and serve.

Italian Style Sausage Stuffed Eggplant

Preparation time: 15 minutes

Cooking time: 55 minutes

Nutrition facts (per serving): 614 Cal (fats 31g, proteins 34.5g, fibers 8.4g)

Ingredients (4 servings)

2 eggplants, halved lengthwise

4 tablespoons of dry breadcrumbs

2 cups of mozzarella cheese

2 tablespoons of olive oil

1 pound of Italian sausage

½ teaspoon of dried Italian seasoning

½ teaspoon of garlic powder

¼ teaspoon of black pepper

4 cups of spaghetti sauce

2 eggs, beaten

Preparation

Brush the eggplants with oil. Place onto a baking sheet with the cut side up and roast in a preheated oven at 400 F for 32-34 minutes. Brown the Italian sausage, season with garlic powder, pepper and Italian seasoning. Stir in the eggs, 1 cup of spaghetti sauce and 1 cup of mozzarella cheese. Scoop out the eggplant flesh, chop and add it into the sausage mixture. Divide the mixture between the eggplants, sprinkle with mozzarella cheese and bake for 32 minutes, or until golden brown. Warm the remaining spaghetti sauce and serve with the eggplants.

Italian Mushrooms

Preparation time: 10 minutes
Cooking time: 4 hours
Nutrition facts (per serving): 99 Cal (fats 8g, proteins 3g, fibers 1g)

Ingredients (6 servings)
½ cup of melted butter
1 envelope of Italian salad dressing mix
1 pound of fresh mushrooms
1 large onion, sliced

Preparation
Layer the mushrooms and onions in a slow cooker. Mix the butter and Italian salad dressing mix, pour it over the vegetables in the slow cooker. Cover and cook on low setting for about 4 hours, or until the vegetables are tender.

Spinach Cheese Casserole

Preparation time: 5 minutes
Cooking time: 15 minutes
Nutrition facts (per serving): 239 Cal (fats 21g, proteins 10g, fibers 3g)

Ingredients (6 servings)

1 cup of grated parmesan cheese

3 garlic cloves, minced

5 tablespoons of butter

2 pounds of baby spinach

3 tablespoons of olive oil

¾ teaspoon of salt

1 tablespoon of Italian seasoning

Preparation

Wilt the spinach in boiling water, drain and set them aside. Heat the butter and oil. Add the garlic, seasoning and salt and cook stirring until tender. Spread the spinach on a prepared baking sheet, sprinkle with butter mixture and cheese and bake in a preheated oven at 400 F for 12 minutes.

Chicken with Bacon

Preparation time: 10 minutes
Cooking time: 15 minutes
Nutrition facts (per serving): 387 Cal (fats 21g, proteins 20g, fibers 6g)

Ingredients (4 quarts)

1 tablespoon of chili powder

6 boneless skinless chicken thighs

4 Oz of green chilies, chopped

1 cup of reduced-sodium chicken broth

20 Oz of frozen corn

12 Oz of cream cheese

1/2 pound of bacon strips, coarsely chopped

2 15-oz cans of black beans, rinsed and drained

2 15-oz cans of white kidney beans, rinsed and drained

2 11-oz cans of diced tomatoes and green chilies

1 teaspoon of minced garlic

1 teaspoon of onion powder

2 cups of shredded cheddar cheese

1 teaspoon of ground cumin

1 Oz of ranch salad dressing mix

1 avocado, cubed

Preparation

Cook the bacon on the sauté setting of the pressure cooker until crispy and set aside. Brown the chicken in bacon drippings, return the bacon, top with corn, beans, diced tomatoes, chilies, broth, chili powder, cumin, onion powder, minced garlic, dressing and cream cheese. Cover and cook for 20 minutes. Stir in the shredded cheddar cheese and serve with avocado.

Sautéed Mushrooms

Preparation time: 10 minutes

Cooking time: 20 minutes

Nutrition facts (per serving): 180 Cal (fats 13g, proteins 3g, fibers 2g)

Ingredients (5 servings)

1 pound of baby Bella mushrooms

1 cup of Italian dressing

1 red capsicum, sliced

1 onion, diced

Salt and pepper

A handful of parsley

Preparation

In a skillet, cook the mushrooms with a little salt until they are browned and set aside. Add the dressing, red pepper and onions in a skillet and bring to a boil. Reduce the heat and stir the salt and pepper in. Serve with a dash of parsley.

Crispy Cauliflower with Garlic Parmesan

Preparation time: 10 minutes

Cooking time: 30 minutes

Nutrition facts (per serving): 247 Cal (fats 18 g, proteins 6g, fibers 1g)

Ingredients (6 servings)

½ cup of melted butter

½ cup of grated parmesan cheese

1 medium-sized cauliflower piece, cut into florets

2 garlic cloves, minced

¼ teaspoon of salt

¼ teaspoon of black pepper

1 cup of plain breadcrumbs

Preparation

Melt the butter and stir the garlic in. Place the cheese, breadcrumbs, pepper and salt in a bowl and mix well. Dip each floret in the butter, then in the breadcrumb mixture. Place the florets on a prepared baking sheet and bake in a preheated oven at 400 F for 32-34 minutes, until golden brown.

Instant Pot Sesame Chicken

Preparation time: 5 minutes
Cooking time: 15 minutes
Nutrition facts (per serving): 311 Cal (fats 9g, proteins 37g, fibers 0g)

Ingredients (4servings)

1 ½ pounds of boneless skinless chicken breasts, cut into 1-inch pieces
¼ tablespoon of crushed red pepper flakes
1 tablespoon of sesame oil
1 tablespoon of sesame seeds
3 tablespoons of corn starch
3 garlic cloves, minced
¼ cup of soy sauce
¼ cup of honey
¼ cup of green onions, thinly sliced
Hot cooked rice
Water

Preparation

Set the pressure cooker on sauté setting. Add the oil, brown the chicken in batches and set aside. In a bowl, whisk the soy sauce, water, honey, pepper flakes and garlic. Return the chicken in the pressure cooker, add the soy mixture in, cover and cook on high pressure for 4-6 minutes, then release the pressure. Mix the cornstarch and water, stir into the chicken and cook stirring on low heat until it thickens. Serve with rice.

Italian Jambalaya Risotto

Preparation time: 15 minutes
Cooking time: 10 minutes
Nutrition facts (per serving): 396 Cal (fats 18 g, Proteins 24 g, fibers 2g)

Ingredients (8 servings)

½ pound of boneless skinless chicken breasts, cut into 1-inch pieces

1 tablespoon of Cajun seasoning

1 pound of cooked andouille sausage, cut into small slices

¾ cup of shredded parmesan cheese

1 ½ cups of Arborio rice

½ cup of dry white wine

2 14-oz cans of chicken broth

2 garlic cloves, minced

1 large green pepper, chopped

1 large green onion, diced

2 plum tomatoes, seeded and chopped

½ cup of chopped celery

¼ teaspoon of pepper

1/3 cup of chopped parsley leaves

2 tablespoons of canola oil

Salt and black pepper

Preparation

Brown the sausage with 1 tablespoon of oil in a pressure cooker set at sauté mode and set aside. Season the chicken with Cajun seasoning, cook stirring in the pressure cooker for 6-7 minutes and set aside. Cook the onions, green pepper, garlic and celery in 1 tablespoon of hot oil. Stir the rice in, add the wine and broth and cook on high pressure for 5 minutes. Release the pressure and stir in the sausage, tomatoes, chicken, parsley and pepper. Cook until ready, garnish with cheese and parsley, and then spoon over spaghetti.

Italian Parmesan Tilapia

Preparation time: 10 minutes

Cooking time: 25 minutes

Nutrition facts (per serving): 592 Cal (fats 124.5g, Proteins 39.4g, fibers 2.2g)

Ingredients (4 servings)

4 of 4-oz tilapia fillets

1 cup of grated parmesan cheese

4 tablespoons of melted butter

1 ½ cups of seasoned breadcrumbs

Preparation

Preheat the oven at 375 F. Mix the breadcrumbs and cheese. Melt the butter, dip the tilapia fillets in it and dredge them in the cheese mixture. Bake in the oven for 25-30 minutes.

Milanese Pork with Rice

Preparation time: 20 minutes
Cooking time: 40 minutes

Ingredients

1 cup of cooked pork, cubed
1/2 cup of chopped sweet red pepper
1/2 cup of uncooked instant rice
1 cup of fresh mushrooms, sliced
1/3 cup of chopped onions
1 garlic clove, minced
1 tablespoon of butter
1 (14.5 ounce) can of Italian diced tomatoes, undrained
1/2 cup of chopped green pepper
1 teaspoon of Italian seasoning
1/2 teaspoon of salt
1 pinch of sugar

Preparation

In a saucepan, sauté the onions, mushrooms and garlic in butter until tender. Stir in the Italian seasoning, tomatoes, pork, peppers and salt if desired. Add sugar and bring to a boil. Stir the rice in. Cover, remove from the heat and let it sit for 7 minutes. Stir before serving.

Venice Fish Fillets

Preparation time: 20 minutes
Cooking time: 35 minutes

Ingredients

1 medium green or yellow bell pepper, julienned
1 small onion, julienned
1/2 cup of fat free Italian salad dressing
1/2 teaspoon of Italian seasoning
2 (14.5 ounce) cans of diced tomatoes
1 1/2 pounds of fresh or frozen cod fillets, thawed

Preparation

In a large nonstick skillet, cook the onions, green peppers, salad dressing and Italian seasoning for 6-7 minutes, or until the vegetables are tender. Stir the tomatoes in and add the fillets. Bring to a boil. Reduce the heat; cover and simmer for 11-13 minutes, or until the fish flakes easily with a fork. Serve with a slotted spoon.

Italian Turkey Burger

Preparation time: 10 minutes

Cooking time: 25 minutes

Nutrition facts (per serving): 235 Cal (fats 11.5g, proteins 28.3g, fibers 0.4g)

Ingredients (4 servings)

1 pound of ground turkey

¼ cup of Italian seasoned breadcrumbs

1 teaspoon of pepper

¼ cup of grated parmesan cheese

Preparation

Mix all the ingredients in a bowl. Shape into 4 patties and bake in a preheated oven at 400 F until brown. Serve with a vegetable salad.

Pasta

Cheesy Sicilian Tortellini

Preparation time: 20 minutes
Cooking time: 7 hours 18 minutes

Ingredients

1/2 pound of ground beef

1/2 pound of Italian sausage, casings removed

1 16-oz jar of marinara sauce

1 4.5-oz can of sliced mushrooms

1 14.5-oz can of Italian-style diced tomatoes, undrained

1 9-oz package of cheese tortellini

1 cup of shredded mozzarella cheese

1/2 cup of shredded cheddar cheese

Preparation

Crumble the Italian sausage and ground beef into a large skillet. Cook over a medium-high heat until browned and drain. Combine the ground meats, marinara sauce, mushrooms and tomatoes in a slow cooker. Cook covered on low heat for 7 hours. Stir the tortellini in. Sprinkle the cheddar and mozzarella cheese over the top. Cover and cook for an additional 14-18 minutes, or until the tortellini are tender.

Truffle Pasta

Preparation time: 5 minutes
Cooking time: 10 minutes
Nutrition facts (per serving): 721 Cal (fats 31g, Proteins 24g, Fibers 4g)

Ingredients (4 servings)
8 Oz of pasta
1 Oz of fresh black truffle
½ stick of unsalted butter
½ cup of grated parmesan cheese
Salt and pepper
Fresh parsley

Preparation
Cook the pasta in salted boiling water according to the instructions on the package. Drain and reserve the liquid. Stir ¾ of grated black truffle in melted butter. Stir the pasta into the butter. Add ¼ cup of the pasta water and cook on low heat. Add the cheese, garnish with parsley and black truffle.

Capers Anchovies Spaghetti

Preparation time: 15 minutes

Cooking time: 20 minutes

Nutrition facts (per serving): 396 Cal (fats 19g, Proteins 13g, fibers 6g)

Ingredients (4 servings)

1 onion, finely chopped

3 tablespoons of olive oil

2 tablespoons of drained capers

5 anchovy fillets, finely chopped

2 garlic cloves, minced

½ teaspoon of chili flakes

120 black olives, pitted

12 Oz of spaghetti

Parsley to taste

Preparation

Fry the onions with oil. Add a pinch of salt, garlic and chili. Stir the capers, anchovies and olives in. Fry for about 14-16 minutes, then season to taste. Cook the spaghetti in salty boiling water, drain and toss with the sauce and parsley.

Baked Broccoli Cheese Pasta

Preparation time: 10 minutes
Cooking time: 20 minutes
Nutrition facts (per serving): 539 Cal (fats 21g, Proteins 25g, Fibers 5g)

Ingredients (4 servings)

1 Oz (25g) of butter
5 Oz (140g) of grated cheddar
10 Oz (280g) of penne
10 Oz (280g) of broccoli florets
1 ¼ cups (300ml) of milk
¼ cup (32g) of flour
1 tablespoon of wholegrain mustard

Preparation

Cook the pasta according to the instructions on the package. Add the broccoli and cook until tender. Heat the butter and stir in the flour, add the milk and bring to a boil. Simmer and add the mustard, cheese and seasoning in. Mix the pasta, sauce and broccoli and grill until golden.

Baked Cheese and Chicken Pasta

Preparation time: 30 minutes

Cooking time: 40 minutes

Nutrition facts (per serving): 575 Cal (fats 30g, Proteins 33g, fibers 5g)

Ingredients (6 servings)

2 14-oz (400g) cans of diced tomatoes

4 tablespoons of olive oil

2 Oz (50g) of grated mozzarella

¼ teaspoon of chili flakes

4 skinless chicken breasts, sliced

1 onion, finely chopped

2 garlic cloves, minced

1 ½ Oz (70g) of grated cheddar

1 teaspoon of caster sugar

6 tablespoons of mascarpone

11 Oz (300g) of penne

Parsley to taste

Preparation

Sauté the onions in oil, add the garlic and chili and cook for 1 minute. Add the tomatoes and sugar and season to taste. Simmer until it thickens, then stir the mascarpone in. Season the chicken and fry it in oil. Cook the penne, drain and toss it with oil. Add the pasta into a bowl, stir in the chicken and pour the sauce in. Top with parsley, mozzarella and cheddar and bake for 21-24 minutes at 220 F, or until golden.

Baked Tuna Pasta

Preparation time: 30 minutes
Cooking time: 40 minutes
Nutrition facts (per serving): 752 Cal (fats 26g, Proteins 37g, fibers 4g)

Ingredients (6 servings)

2 ½ cups (600ml) of milk

8-oz can of sweet corn

½ cup (60g) of flour

20 Oz (600g) of rigatoni

¼ cup of butter

8 Oz of grated cheddar

2 cans of tuna steak, drained

Some chopped parsley

Preparation

Cook the rigatoni, drain and set aside. Melt the butter, stir the flour in and cook for 1 minute. Add in the milk and cook stirring to make a white sauce. Remove from the heat and stir ½ of the cheddar, tuna, pasta, 1 can of sweet corn and parsley in. Season and transfer into a baking dish, then top with cheddar. Bake for about 22 minutes until the cheese is golden.

Spaghetti Meatballs

Preparation time: 30 minutes
Cooking time: 30 minutes
Nutrition facts (per serving): 870 Cal (fats 37g, Proteins 46g, Fibers 5g)

Ingredients (8 servings)

2 pounds of minced beef

8 pork sausages

A bunch of parsley, finely chopped

1 onion, finely chopped

4 Oz of grated parmesan cheese

1 cup of breadcrumbs

2 eggs, beaten

4 garlic cloves, minced

½ tablespoon of oil

3 tablespoons of caster sugar

4 14-oz cans of chopped tomatoes

Preparation

Skin the sausages into a bowl and add the minced beef, ½ of the parsley, eggs, onions, 3 Oz of parmesan, breadcrumbs and seasoning. Mash, make the balls and drizzle with oil. Roast them for 28-32 minutes or until browned. Heat 3 tablespoons of oil. Cook the garlic, stir in the tomatoes, wine, sugar and parsley to make a sauce. Serve the balls with the sauce.

Zucchini Bacon Pasta

Preparation time: 10 minutes

Cooking time: 20 minutes

Nutrition facts (per serving): 483 Cal (fats 18.4g, Proteins 21.5g, fibers 3.8g)

Ingredients (4 servings)

7 Oz (200g) of low-fat crème Fraiche

A handful of grated parmesan

1 tablespoon of olive oil

4 Oz of pancetta, diced

4 zucchinis, coarsely grated

1 garlic clove, minced

10 Oz (300g) of tagliatelle

Preparation

Fry the pancetta in oil for 5-6 minutes or until it starts to crisp. Add the zucchinis. Cook until soft, add the garlic, cook for 1 minute and set aside. Cook the tagliatelle and add it into the bacon mixture. Toss with crème Fraiche and parmesan over low heat, season, sprinkle with cheese and serve.

New Kale and Pesto Pasta

Preparation time: 25 minutes

Cooking time: 10 minutes

Nutrition facts (per serving): 428 Cal (fats 13g, Proteins 17g, fibers 11g)

Ingredients (4 servings)

7 Oz (200g) of whole meal pasta

4 tablespoons of pesto

1 tablespoon of rapeseed oil

2 red onions, thinly sliced

10 Oz (300g) of kale

4 tablespoons of cream cheese

Preparation

Sauté the onions until soft, add the kale in and cook until they wilt. Cook the pasta, drain and toss in the kale mixture. Add the pesto, cheese and some water in if needed. Season and serve.

Courgette Lasagna

Preparation time: 10 minutes
Cooking time: 20 minutes
Nutrition facts (per serving): 405 Cal (fats 21g, Proteins 18g, Fibers 4g)

Ingredients (4 servings)

9 dried lasagna sheets
1 tablespoon of oil
1 onion, finely chopped
2 garlic cloves, minced
6 zucchinis, coarsely grated
8-oz (250g) tub of ricotta
½ cup of cheddar cheese
12 Oz of tomato sauce

Preparation

Cook the lasagna sheets in boiling water until soft. Rinse in cold water and drizzle with oil. Sauté the onion, add the garlic and zucchini and cook until soft. Stir 2/3 of cheddar and ricotta in, then season. Heat the tomato sauce until hot. Layer the lasagna in a baking dish and add half of the zucchini mixture, pasta and tomato sauce. Repeat for another layer, top with blobs of ricotta and sprinkle the cheese. Bake until the pasta is tender and the cheddar is golden.

Vegetarian Caponata Pasta

Preparation time: 5 minutes
Cooking time: 20 minutes
Nutrition facts (per serving): 542 Cal (fats 14g, Proteins 14g, Fibers 9g)

Ingredients (4 servings)
4 tablespoons of olive oil
1 large onion, finely chopped
4 garlic cloves, minced
12 Oz of rigatoni or penne
1 tablespoon of small capers
14-oz can of diced tomatoes
8 Oz (250g) of char-grilled Mediterranean veg, roughly chopped
2 tablespoons of raisins
Some parmesan
A bunch of basil leaves

Preparation
Fry the onions until tender, add the garlic and cook for 1 minute. Add in the raisins, tomatoes, mixed vegetables and capers. Season and simmer until the sauce thickens. Cook the pasta and drain, mix it with the sauce, sprinkle with basil leaves and parmesan.

Italian Macaroni and Cheese

Preparation time: 10 minutes

Cooking time: 40 minutes

Nutrition facts (per serving): 860 Cal (fats 42g, Proteins 38g, fibers 0g)

Ingredients (4 servings)

12 Oz of short spiral pasta

8 Oz (250g) of grated vegetarian cheddar

½ cup of baguette, chopped into small chunks

3 tablespoons of butter

1 teaspoon of mustard powder

3 tablespoons of flour

2 cups (500ml) of milk

¼ cup of grated parmesan

Preparation

Spread the baguette on a baking sheet and drizzle with 1 tablespoon of melted butter. Season and bake until crispy. Cook the pasta, drain and set aside. Melt the butter. Cook the garlic and mustard, stir the flour and milk in, cook for 1 minute and simmer until it thickens. Take it off of the heat, add cheddar and parmesan and stir the pasta in. Season, sprinkle with parmesan and bake until golden.

Creamy Fettuccine Alfredo

Preparation time: 15 minutes
Cooking time: 10 minutes
Nutrition facts (per serving): 898 Cal (fats 67g, Proteins 23g, Fibers 3g)

Ingredients (2 servings)

½ cup of grated parmesan

9 Oz of fettuccine

8-oz tub of clotted cream

2 tablespoons of butter

1 tablespoon of corn flour

Some grated nutmeg

Preparation

In a pan, on low heat, combine the cream, butter and flour. Simmer for 5 minutes and set aside. Mix the cheese and nutmeg in a bowl, stir in some black pepper and set aside. Cook the pasta in salted boiling water, drain and add the pasta in the cream mixture. Sprinkle and fold in the cheese over low heat. Add 3 tablespoons of the drained pasta water and cook stirring until the sauce is glossy. Season, sprinkle with parsley and serve.

Mushroom Bacon Pasta

Preparation time: 5 minutes
Cooking time: 20 minutes
Nutrition facts (per serving): 567 Cal (fats 20g, Proteins 23g, fibers 4g)

Ingredients (4 servings)

14 Oz of penne pasta
8-oz (250g) package of button mushrooms, sliced
4 tablespoons of pesto
8 rashers of streaky bacon, cut into small pieces
A handful of basil leaves
¾ cup (180ml) of crème Fraiche

Preparation

Cook the pasta in salted boiling water, drain and set aside. Fry the bacon and mushrooms until golden. Add the pasta and some water in and cook stirring for 2 minutes. Take it off of the heat and spoon the pesto and crème Fraiche in. Add basil and stir. Sprinkle with basil and serve.

Spicy Spaghetti with Mushrooms

Preparation time: 10 minutes
Cooking time: 15 minutes
Nutrition facts (per serving): 346 Cal (fats 7g, proteins 12g, fibers 5g)

Ingredients (4 servings)

12 Oz of spaghetti
8-oz (250g) package of chestnut mushrooms, thinly sliced
1 garlic clove, minced
1 onion, finely chopped
14-oz can of diced tomatoes
½ deseeded red chili, finely chopped
2 tablespoons of olive oil
1 celery, finely chopped
A bunch of parsley

Preparation

Fry the mushrooms with 1 tablespoon of oil until soft and golden. Fry the garlic in, add some parsley and set aside. Fry the onion and celery until slightly brown, stir the tomatoes, salt and chili in, bring to a boil and simmer until it thickens. Boil the spaghetti according to the instructions on the package and drain. Toss with the sauce and top with the mushrooms.

Italian Linguine with Avocado

Preparation time: 20 minutes
Cooking time: 10 minutes
Nutrition facts (per serving): 450 Cal (fats 20g, Proteins 11g, fibers 13g)

Ingredients (4 servings)
8 Oz (230g) of whole meal linguine
2 medium-sized avocados, chopped
4 ripe tomatoes, chopped
1 red chili, deseeded and chopped
Juice and zest of 1 ½ lime
1 pack of chopped fresh coriander
2 small red onions, finely chopped

Preparation
Cook the pasta in boiling water until soft. Into a bowl, mix the avocado, zest, lime juice, tomatoes, onion, chili and coriander. Drain the pasta, toss it with the avocado mixture and serve.

Italian Pesto Spaghetti with Artichokes

Preparation time: 5 minutes
Cooking time: 15 minutes
Nutrition facts (per serving): 565 Cal (fats 24g, Proteins 22g, fibers 6g)

Ingredients (4 servings)

12 Oz of spaghetti

2 eggs

14-oz can of drained and dried artichokes

2 tablespoons of milk

¼ cup of parmesan cheese

4 tablespoons of green pesto

¼ cup of pine nuts

Preparation

Cook the spaghetti in salty boiling water until soft, drain and set aside. Into a bowl, mix the artichokes, eggs, milk, pesto, parmesan and seasoning. Toast the nuts in a pan until pale golden. Add the drained pasta into a pan, add the egg mixture, then toss and cook on low heat. Sprinkle with parmesan and serve.

Spaghetti Pea Pesto

Preparation time: 10 minutes
Cooking time: 15 minutes
Nutrition facts (per serving): 512 Cal (fats 18g, Proteins 26g, Fibers 7g)

Ingredients (4 servings)

12 Oz of spaghetti
7-oz (190g) package of cooked prawns
14 Oz of frozen peas
4-oz tub of garlic and soft herb cheese
Juice and zest of 1 lemon
1 garlic clove, minced

Preparation

Whizz the peas with lemon zest, soft cheese, lemon juice and garlic, season and set aside. Cook the spaghetti in salty boiling water, add the remaining peas and cook for about 2 minutes. Drain and return the pasta in the pan, stir the pea pesto in and season. Serve with the prawns.

Currant Fennel Spaghetti

Preparation time: 15 minutes
Cooking time: 15 minutes
Nutrition facts (per serving): 579 Cal (fats 23g, Proteins 17g, fibers 7g)

Ingredients (4 servings)

14 Oz of spaghetti

3-oz jar of anchovy fillets, roughly chopped

2 ½ tablespoons of rinsed capers

2 ½ tablespoons of olive oil

2 quartered fennel bulbs

3 garlic cloves, finely sliced

½ teaspoon of dried chili flakes

3 Oz of currants, soaked and drained

3 Oz of pine nuts, toasted

1 lemon juice

Parsley leaves to taste

Preparation

Remove the core and hard skin of the fennel and chop. Cook the spaghetti in salty boiling water, according to the instructions on the package. Sauté the fennel until soft, add the garlic and cook for 7 minutes, or until cooked. Stir in the anchovies and chili. Toss the currants, parsley, capers, and some pine nuts in. Add the pasta and lemon juice into a pan and season. Toss and sprinkle with the remaining pine nuts and fennel. Serve with the currants mixture.

Bow Ties with Tomatoes and Sausage

Preparation time: 15 minutes
Cooking time: 40 minutes
Nutrition facts (per serving): 656 Cal (fats 42.1g, proteins 20.1g, fibers 3.4g)

Ingredients (4 servings)

12-oz package of bowtie pasta

1 pound of crumbled Italian sausage

28 Oz of plum tomatoes, drained, chopped

½ cup of diced onion

½ teaspoon of red pepper flakes

2 tablespoons of olive oil

3 tablespoons of minced parsley

½ teaspoon of salt

1 ½ cups of heavy cream

Preparation

Cook the pasta in salted boiling water, according to the instructions on the package. Drain when finished. Cook the crumbled sausage and pepper flakes in oil until the sausage browns. Stir the onion and garlic in and cook until tender. Add the cream, tomatoes and salt. Cook stirring for about 8 minutes. Stir the pasta in the sauce and sprinkle with parsley.

Pasta with Spinach and Bacon

Preparation time: 10 minutes

Cooking time: 15 minutes

Nutrition facts (per serving): 517 Cal (fats 14.8g, proteins 21g, fibers 6.6g)

Ingredients (4 servings)

6 slices of bacon, chopped

12 Oz of penne pasta

1 bunch of fresh spinach, cut into smaller pieces

2 tablespoons of olive oil

14-oz can of diced tomatoes

2 tablespoons of minced garlic

Preparation

Cook the pasta according to the instructions on the package and set aside. Brown the beef in 1 tablespoon of oil, add the garlic and cook for 2 minutes, then stir in the tomatoes. Add the spinach to coriander and run boiling water through them to wilt them. Drain the pasta and spinach, toss both with oil. Add the bacon and garlic mixture.

Dips and Appetizers

Sausage and Cheese Dip

Preparation time: 10 minutes

Cooking time: 35 minutes

Nutrition facts (per serving): 70 Cal (fats 6g, proteins 3g, fibers 0g)

Ingredients (48 servings)

¾ pound of sausage

1 tablespoon of Italian seasoning

3 garlic cloves, minced

8 Oz of smoked Gouda, cubed

$^1/_3$ cup of mayonnaise

$^1/_3$ cup of sour cream

8 Oz of crumbled cheddar cheese

Preparation

Preheat the oven to 350 F. Brown the sausage and add the cheese. Spread the sausage on a greased baking dish, sprinkle with seasoning. Top with the sour cream, garlic and mayonnaise. Add the cheese on top. Bake in the oven for 28-31 minutes, with occasional stirring after every 10 minutes, until the cheese melts.

Eggplant Spread

Preparation time: 20 minutes

Cooking time: 50 minutes

Nutrition facts (per serving): 84 Cal (fats 5g, proteins 1g, fibers 3g)

Ingredients

1 tablespoon of tomato paste

3 garlic cloves, minced

3 tablespoons of olive oil

½ teaspoon of salt

½ teaspoon of pepper

2 large red peppers, chopped

1 medium-sized eggplant, chopped

1 medium-sized onion thinly sliced

Toasted baguette slices

Preparation

Preheat the oven to 400 F. Mix the garlic, oil, salt and pepper in a bowl. Add the vegetables in the dish and toss them with the garlic mixture. Roast in the oven for 38-42 minutes. Stir after 20 minutes. Transfer in a blender, cool slightly, add the tomato paste and blend the mixture. Serve with the toasted baguette slices.

Italian Hoagie Dip

Preparation time: 20 minutes

Nutrition facts (per serving): 374 Cal (fats 30g, proteins 18g, fibers 3g)

Ingredients (8 servings)

8 slices of provolone cheese, diced

1 tablespoon of Italian seasoning

3 cups of romaine lettuce, finely chopped

¼ pound of diced deli ham

¼ pound of Genoa salami

¼ pound of diced pepperoni

½ cup of diced onions

½ cup of mayonnaise

Preparation

In a bowl, combine the meats, onions and cheese. Stir the mayonnaise and Italian seasoning in. Stir in the lettuce and serve with crackers.

Italian Creamy Dip

Preparation time: 5 minutes
Nutrition facts (per serving): 53 Cal (fats 30g, proteins 1g, fibers 0g)

Ingredients (8 servings)

$^1/_8$ teaspoon of onion powder

1 cup of sour cream

½ teaspoon of garlic salt

¼ teaspoon of Italian seasoning

Preparation

Mix all the ingredients in a bowl. Refrigerate for about 70 minutes for the flavors to blend and serve.

Rosemary Baked Olives and Orange

Preparation time: 25 minutes

Cooking time: 15 minutes

Nutrition facts (per serving): 75 Cal (fats 7.5g, proteins 0.7g, fibers 0.5g)

Ingredients (12 servings)

2 ½ teaspoons of chopped oregano

¼ teaspoon of crushed red pepper flakes

3 ½ cups of whole mixed olives

2 tablespoons of orange juice

¼ cup of dry white wine

2 garlic cloves, minced

2 tablespoons of olive oil

2 sprigs of rosemary

2 tablespoons of chopped parsley

2 tablespoons of grated orange zest

Preparation

Preheat the oven to 375 F. Add the wine, olives, olive oil, garlic and orange juice in a baking dish and stir. Nestle the rosemary in the olive mixture and bake in the oven for 14-17 minutes. Stir after 8 minutes. Remove the rosemary; stir the parsley, zest, pepper and oregano in. Serve while warm.

Mozzarella Tomato Bites

Preparation time: 30 minutes
Cooking time: 30 minutes
Nutrition facts (per serving): 225 Cal (fats 17.9g, proteins 9.4g, fibers 0.5g)

Ingredients (8 servings)

20 small balls of mozzarella cheese
20 cherry tomatoes, halved
20 basil leaves
20 toothpicks
½ cup of balsamic vinegar
¼ cup of olive oil
Salt and pepper

Preparation

With a toothpick, spear the half of a tomato, basil leaf, cheese and another half of the tomato. Repeat the process with the other ingredients and place them on a serving dish. Sprinkle with salt and pepper. Add the oil and vinegar in a small bowl to serve as a dip to taste.

Battered Calamari

Preparation time: 10 minutes

Cooking time: 5 minutes

Nutrition facts (per serving): 209 Cal (fats 8.6g, proteins 13.9g, fibers 0.8g)

Ingredients (6 servings)

1 cup of buttermilk

2 cups of vegetable oil

1 pound of squid, cut into rings

½ tablespoon of ground black pepper

1 cup of flour

½ tablespoon of salt

1 teaspoon of dried oregano

Preparation

Combine the flour, pepper, salt and oregano in a bowl. Add the buttermilk into another bowl and dip in the squid rings, then dip them into the flour mixture. Deep-fry the coated pieces in hot oil in batches until they are evenly browned. Place them on a paper towel to drain and serve.

Italian Strawberry Bruschetta

Preparation time: 10 minutes

Cooking time: 5 minutes

Nutrition facts (per serving): 120 Cal (fats 1.6g, proteins 3.7g, fibers 1.2g)

Ingredients (12 servings)

24 slices of baguette

1 tablespoon of softened butter

2 cups of fresh strawberries, chopped

¼ cup of white sugar

Preparation

Preheat the oven. Spread the butter on each slice of bread. Arrange the bread slices on a baking sheet and broil for 2 minutes. Add the strawberries on each toast, sprinkle with sugar and cook for another 3 minutes until the sugar caramelizes and serve.

Salads

Italian Roasted Tomato Salad

Preparation time: 25 minutes

Cooking time: 20 minutes

Nutrition facts (per serving): 157 Cal (fats 10.9g, proteins 7.1g, fibers 2.1g)

Ingredients (6 servings)

3 tomatoes, wedged

3 garlic cloves, minced

1 onion, thinly sliced

3 tablespoons of sliced basil leaves

½ teaspoon of dried marjoram

4 lettuce leaves, thinly sliced

3 Oz of grated parmesan cheese

½ teaspoon of dried oregano

Leaves from 1 piece of Boston lettuce

1 tablespoon of balsamic vinegar

3 tablespoons of vinegar

Salt and black pepper

Preparation

Preheat the oven to 350 F. Mix the garlic, onion, tomatoes, oregano, marjoram and basil leaves in a baking dish. Sprinkle with pepper and salt. Drizzle with oil and balsamic vinegar and toss. Roast in the oven for 28-32 minutes and set aside. Serve with Boston and romaine lettuce and top with cheese.

Spicy Italian Salad

Preparation time: 4 hours
Nutrition facts (per serving): 248 Cal (fats 21.1g, proteins 3.6g, fibers 3.7g)

Ingredients (6 servings)

½ cup of canola oil

1/3 cup of tarragon vinegar

8-oz can of artichoke hearts, drained and quartered

½ cup of pitted green olives

¼ cup of black olives

2 garlic cloves, minced

1 tablespoon of chopped fresh thyme

1 tablespoon of white sugar

5 cups of romaine lettuce, rinsed and drained

½ teaspoon of dry mustard

1 red bell pepper, sliced

1 carrot, grated

1 red onion, thinly sliced

Ground pepper

2 tablespoons of grated romaine cheese

½ cucumber, sliced

Preparation

Add the vinegar, sugar, oil, garlic, thyme and mustard in a large container with a lid. Cover and shake to mix. Place the artichoke hearts in the container mixture, cover and marinate. Keep refrigerated for at least 4 hours. In a bowl, toss the bell peppers, carrots, cucumber, lettuce, onion, olives and cheese. Season and pour the artichoke mixture in, toss to coat.

Italian Bocconcini Salad

Preparation time: 20 minutes
Nutrition facts (per serving): 448 Cal (fats 35.7g, proteins 25.9g, fibers 1.2g)

Ingredients (4 servings)

1 pound of bite-sized mozzarella balls

½ cup of arugula, coarsely chopped

8 cherry tomatoes

½ cup of green peppers, chopped

2 tablespoons of basil leaves, chopped

½ cup of celery, chopped

½ cup of Belgian endive leaves

Salt and black pepper

1 ½ tablespoons of fresh lemon juice

3 tablespoons of extra virgin oil

Preparation

In a bowl, combine the mozzarella, arugula, tomatoes, bell peppers, celery and endive. In a small bowl, whisk the oil and lemon juice, pour the mixture over the salad and toss well. Place on individual plates, sprinkle with basil leaves, season with salt and pepper, then serve.

Zucchini Orzo Salad

Preparation time: 15 minutes

Cooking time: 15 minutes

Nutrition facts (per serving): 236 Cal (fats 5.6g, proteins 7.7g, fibers 2.3g)

Ingredients (4 servings)

2 zucchinis, quartered lengthwise and sliced

1 cup of orzo

4 teaspoons of olive oil

1 garlic clove, chopped

1 tablespoon of white wine

½ cup of fresh basil leaves

Salt and ground pepper

Preparation

Cook the orzo in salted boiling water until cooked through and drain. Spread them on a baking sheet and cool. Cook the zucchini in 1 tablespoon of hot oil until tender and season with salt and pepper. Mix the vinegar, orzo, basil, 1 tablespoon of oil and orzo in a bowl and cover using a wrap. Refrigerate for an hour before serving.

Arugula and Parmesan Salad

Preparation time: 20 minutes
Nutrition facts (per serving): 54 Cal (fats 3.2g, proteins 3.9g, fibers 1.5g)

Ingredients (4 servings)

2 5-oz packages of arugula

1 teaspoon of red pepper flakes

¼ cup of shredded parmesan cheese

1 tablespoon of olive oil

1 teaspoon of balsamic vinegar

¼ cup of chopped cilantro

1 teaspoon of olive oil

A pinch of black pepper

Preparation

In a large salad bowl, toss the arugula and cilantro, drizzle with vinegar, olive oil and lemon juice. Sprinkle with red and black pepper and toss. Sprinkle with parmesan and serve.

Mozzarella and Tomato Salad

Preparation time: 15 minutes

Nutrition facts (per serving): 311 Cal (fats 23.9g, proteins 17.9g, fibers 1.5g)

Ingredients (6 servings)

1 pound of mozzarella cheese, sliced

4 large tomatoes, sliced

$1/3$ cup of basil leaves

3 tablespoons of olive oil

Salt and pepper

Preparation

On a platter, alternate the tomato slices with cheese slices and basil. Drizzle with oil and season with salt and pepper.

Confetti Pasta Salad

Preparation time: 20 minutes
Nutrition facts (per serving): 354 Cal (fats 30.9g, proteins 3.4g, fibers 1.5g)

Ingredients (6 servings)
1 tablespoon of white wine
1 cup of mayonnaise
1 garlic clove, minced
2 cups of rotini pasta (other types of pasta are good too)
½ cup of black olives, sliced
½ cup of yellow bell peppers, chopped
¼ teaspoon of ground black pepper
1 tablespoon of salt
1 ½ tablespoons of fresh basil, chopped
1 cup of tomatoes, chopped

Preparation
Cook the pasta in salty water, according to the instructions. When soft, rinse and drain. In a salad bowl, whisk the salt, mayonnaise, black pepper, vinegar and garlic. Add the basil, olives, tomatoes and bell peppers and mix well. Keep chilled for hours before serving.

Italian Feta Cheese Salad

Preparation time: 10 minutes

Nutrition facts (per serving): 131 Cal (fats 10.1g, proteins 3.2g, fibers 1.6g)

Ingredients (2 servings)

3 tablespoons of crumbled feta cheese

½ onion, diced

1 tablespoon of lemon juice

12 cherry tomatoes, thinly sliced

1 tablespoon of oil

Preparation

In a bowl, mix the tomatoes, cheese, onion, oil and lemon juice. Serve immediately.

Soups

Italian Buttery Onion Soup

Preparation time: 5 minutes

Cooking time: 30 minutes

Nutrition facts (per serving): 294 Cal (fats 23g, proteins 11g, fibers 1g)

Ingredients (6 servings)

2 cups of shredded mozzarella cheese

2 cups of milk

½ cup of cubed butter

¼ cup of flour

2 cups of thinly sliced onions

2 cups of chicken broth

Salt and pepper

Preparation

Sauté the onions with butter until tender. Stir in the flour. Add the broth and milk and cook on a medium heat. Add the cheese and stir continuously until it melts. Season with salt and pepper.

Italian Vegan Vegetable Soup

Preparation time: 10 minutes

Cooking time: 35 minutes

Nutrition facts (per serving): 185 Cal (fats 37.2g, proteins 9.1g, fibers 9.5g)

Ingredients (4 servings)

2 14-oz cans of vegetable broth

2 garlic cloves, minced

1/3 cup of frozen pearl onions

15 Oz of drained kidney beans

3 small zucchinis, cubed

1 cube of vegetable bouillon

½ cup of macaroni

1 tablespoon of dried parsley

¾ teaspoon of dried basil

1 bay leaf

28 Oz of peeled, crushed tomatoes

½ cup of frozen green beans

2 large carrots, coarsely grated

1 celery stalk

Preparation

Add the celery, tomatoes, garlic, carrots, green beans, onions, basil, bay leaf, bouillon cube and broth in a saucepan. Bring to a boil, cover and simmer for 14-17 minutes. Stir the macaroni, zucchini and kidney beans in, bring to a boil and simmer for another 15 minutes. Remove the bay leaf and serve.

Hearty Italian Venison Soup

Preparation time: 10 minutes
Cooking time: 160 minutes
Nutrition facts (per serving): 253 Cal (fats 2.7g, proteins 20.9g, fibers 5.9g)

Ingredients (8 servings)

1 pound of ground venison
15-oz can of green beans
15-oz can of pinto beans
14-oz can of stewed tomatoes
8 Oz of any spiral pasta
2 teaspoons of dried oregano
1 onion, chopped
2 teaspoons of dried basil
1 tablespoon of minced garlic
2 8-oz cans of tomato sauce
3 cups of water
1 carrot, chopped
½ teaspoon of salt
1 zucchini, chopped

Preparation

In a skillet, brown the garlic, onion and venison. Add the tomato sauce, tomatoes, water and spices. Bring to a boil and simmer for 27-32 minutes. Stir the zucchini and carrots in. Simmer for 85-95 minutes. Add the pasta, cook until tender, top with cheese and serve.

Italian Sausage and Kale Soup

Preparation time: 10 minutes
Cooking time: 50 minutes
Nutrition facts (per serving): 266 Cal (fats 18g, proteins 10.6g, fibers 1.5g)

Ingredients (12 servings)

1-pound bulk of Italian sausage
1 onion, chopped
4 cups of half-and-half
2 cups of milk
3 cups of cubed potatoes
2 cups of chicken broth
½ teaspoon of ground black pepper
2 cups of kale, bite-sized pieces
½ teaspoon of dried oregano
½ teaspoon of red pepper flakes

Preparation

Crumble the sausage in a saucepan and cook until browned. Drain the excess grease. Stir the half-and-half, onion, red pepper, chicken broth, potatoes, milk and oregano in. Bring to a boil. Simmer for 28-32 minutes and season with black pepper. Add the kale and cook until tender.

Tortellini Sausage Soup

Preparation time: 20 minutes
Cooking time: 75 minutes
Nutrition facts (per serving): 324 Cal (fats 20.2g, proteins 14.6g, fibers 3.1g)

Ingredients (8 servings)

8 Oz of fresh tortellini pasta
1 ½ cups of sliced zucchini
1 pound of Italian sausage
1 cup of carrots, thinly sliced
2 garlic cloves, minced
1 cup of chopped onion
½ tablespoon of packed basil leaves
5 cups of beef broth
½ cup of water
½ cup of red wine
4 tomatoes, peeled, seeded and chopped
3 tablespoons of chopped parsley
8-oz can of tomato sauce
½ teaspoon of dried oregano

Preparation

Brown the sausage, drain and preserve 1 tablespoon of the drippings. Sauté the garlic and onions in the drippings. Stir the broth, water, wine, carrots, tomatoes, basil, oregano, sausage and tomato sauce in. Bring to a boil, cover and simmer for 28-32 minutes. Skim the fat, add the parsley and zucchini. Simmer for 18-22 minutes. Add the tortellini and simmer for 11 minutes. Sprinkle with cheese and serve.

Italian Bean and Kale Soup

Preparation time: 10 minutes
Cooking time: 1hour 20 minutes
Nutrition facts (per serving): 182 Cal (fats 2.5g, proteins 11g, fibers 7.3g)

Ingredients (8 servings)

1 yellow onion, chopped

4 cups of vegetable broth

1 tablespoon of canola oil

8 garlic cloves, minced

4 pieces of kale, chopped

1 cup of chopped parsley

2 15-oz cans of white beans

Salt and pepper

4 plum tomatoes, chopped

Tablespoon of dried Italian herb seasoning

Preparation

Heat the oil in a saucepan and sauté the garlic and onions until soft. Add the kale and cook until they wilt. Add the herbs, 2 cups of beans, 3 cups of broth, tomatoes, salt and pepper and simmer for about 5 minutes. Add the remaining beans and broth into a blender and blend until smooth. Stir the soup in and simmer for a while before serving.

Italian Halibut Soup

Preparation time: 20 minutes
Cooking time: 70 minutes
Nutrition facts (per serving): 262 Cal (fats 10.3g, proteins 31.2g, fibers 2.1g)

Ingredients (8 servings)

2 ½ pounds of cubed halibut steaks

2 16-oz cans of peeled, mashed tomatoes

1 cup of tomato juice

½ cup of apple juice

1 red bell pepper, chopped

1 onion, chopped

3 garlic cloves, minced

3 celery stalks, chopped

¼ cup of olive oil

$1/8$ teaspoon of dried thyme

$1/8$ teaspoon of ground black pepper

½ teaspoon of dried basil

½ teaspoon of salt

2 tablespoons of basil

Preparation

In a pan, sauté the garlic, onion, peppers and celery until soft. Add the apple juice, tomatoes, tomato juice and herbs. Simmer for 28-32 minutes, add the halibut pieces and cook for about 32-34 minutes until done. Then season with salt and pepper.

Ricotta Pie

Preparation time: 15 minutes

Cooking time: 70 minutes

Ingredients

3 pounds of ricotta cheese

12 eggs

2 cups of white sugar

2 teaspoons of vanilla extract

1/4 cup of miniature semisweet chocolate chips

4 cups of all-purpose flour

5 teaspoons of baking powder

1 cup of white sugar

1/2 cup of shortening

4 eggs, lightly beaten

1 teaspoon of vanilla extract

Preparation

Preheat the oven to 325 F. Beat the 12 eggs, 2 cups of sugar and 2 teaspoons of vanilla or lemon extract together. Stir the ricotta cheese and the chocolate chips in. Set aside. Grease two deep dish pie plates. Combine the baking powder, flour and 1 cup of sugar together. Cut the shortening in and mix until the mixture resembles coarse crumbs. Mix in the 4 lightly beaten eggs and 1 teaspoon of the vanilla extract. Divide the dough into 4 balls and chill. Roll out 2 of the balls to fit into the pie pans. Do not make the crust too thick as it will expand during cooking. Do not flute the edges of the dough. Roll out the other 2 balls of dough. Cut each into 8 narrow strips for the top of the crust.

Pour the filling into the pie crusts evenly. Top each pie with 8 narrow strips of dough or cookie cut-outs. Brush the top of the pies with milk. Place foil on the edge of the crust. Bake for 25-35 minutes, then remove the foil. Continue to bake for another 30-32 minutes, or until a knife inserted in the center comes out clean.

Desserts

Venice Love Cake

Preparation time: 20 minutes
Cooking time: 90 minutes

Ingredients

1 18.25-oz package of chocolate cake mix

2 pints of part-skim ricotta cheese

3/4 cup of white sugar

1 teaspoon of vanilla extract

4 eggs

1 3.9-oz package of instant chocolate pudding mix

1 cup of milk

1 12-oz container of frozen whipped topping, thawed

Preparation

Preheat the oven to 350 F. Prepare the cake mix as instructed on the box. Pour the batter into a 9x13x2-inch greased baking dish. Set aside. Combine the sugar, ricotta cheese, vanilla and eggs. Blend well and spread the mixture evenly on top of the cake batter. Bake for 80-90 minutes in a metal pan. Blend the pudding mix and milk until thickened. Blend the whipped topping in and spread over the cooled cake.

Italian Cookies

Preparation time: 15 minutes

Cooking time: 20 minutes

Nutrition facts (per serving): 180 Cal (fats 11g, proteins 3g, fibers 0g)

Ingredients (22 cookies)

1 egg

½ cup of unsalted butter

½ cup of powdered sugar

½ teaspoon of almond extract

½ cup of almond flour

¼ teaspoon of salt

¼ cup of flour

Preparation

Preheat the oven to 350 F. Combine the butter and sugar until light and fluffy, whisk the egg, almond extract and salt in. After a minute, add the flour and almond flour and mix well. Scoop the mixture, roll it in your hands and then press down. Place on a baking tray and bake for 21-24 minutes. Dust with sugar and cool before serving.

Salted Chocolate Brownies

Preparation time: 15 minutes
Cooking time: 25 minutes
Nutrition facts (per serving): 250 Cal (fats 15g, proteins 3g, fibers 2g)

Ingredients (48 servings)

2 eggs
2 teaspoons of vanilla extract
1/3 cup of unsweetened cocoa powder
½ cup of flour
2 teaspoons of turbinado sugar
¼ teaspoon of salt
¾ cup of sugar
½ cup of melted unsalted butter
1 teaspoon of flake salt
½ cup of bittersweet chocolate chunks

Preparation

Preheat the oven to 350 F. In a bowl, whisk the flour, salt and cocoa powder and set aside. In another bowl, whisk the butter, sugar and vanilla. Whisk the eggs in one at a time until the mixture is smooth. Fold in the flour mixture with a rubber spatula. Add more chocolate and fold. Pour the batter into a prepared baking sheet, sprinkle with salt, turbinado sugar and flake salt. Bake for 29-31 minutes and cool before serving.

Espresso Peanut Butter Brownies

Preparation time: 15 minutes
Cooking time: 35 minutes
Nutrition facts (per serving): 150 Cal (fats 8g, proteins 2g, fibers 0g)

Ingredients (24 servings)
1 egg
1/3 cup of vegetable oil
¼ teaspoon of salt
¾ cup of peanut butter chips
2 tablespoons of espresso powder
18 Oz of brownie mix

Preparation
Preheat the oven to 350 F. In a bowl, whisk $^1/_3$ cup of water, oil, egg and espresso powder. Stir the brownie mix in until it blends well. Stir in the peanut butter chips, transfer the batter into a prepared baking pan. Sprinkle with salt evenly and bake for 33-37 minutes. Cut into squares and serve.

Almond and Cherry Cookies

Preparation time: 15 minutes
Cooking time: 30 minutes
Nutrition facts (per serving): 270 Cal (fats 17g, proteins 8g, fibers 4g)

Ingredients (12 servings)

2 tablespoons of limoncello

1 egg

4 cups of almond flour

¼ cup of honey

½ cup of sugar

¼ teaspoon of salt

3 tablespoons of cherry jam

1 teaspoon of lemon zest

Preparation

Preheat the oven to 350 F. Spread 2 cups of almond flour on a rimmed baking sheet. Place in the oven for 15 minutes and stir after 7-9 minutes until brown and toasted. Cool the flour in a bowl, add the remaining flour, honey, sugar, lemon zest, salt, egg and limoncello and combine to form dough. Scoop tablespoon-sized heaping scoops into a prepared baking sheet, flatten slightly and make a small indent on each cookie. Fill each cookie with ½ teaspoon of cherry jam and bake for 14-17 minutes. Allow to cool and serve.

If you liked Italian food, discover to how cook DELICIOUS recipes from neighboring Balkan countries!

Within these pages, you'll learn 35 authentic recipes from a Balkan cook. These aren't ordinary recipes you'd find on the Internet, but recipes that were closely guarded by our Balkan mothers and passed down from generation to generation.

Main Dishes, Appetizers, and Desserts included!

If you want to learn how to make Croatian green peas stew, and 32 other authentic Balkan recipes, then start with our book!

Order at Amazon for only $2,99

If you're a Mediterranean dieter who wants to know the secrets of the Mediterranean diet, dieting, and cooking, then you're about to discover how to master cooking meals on a Mediterranean diet right now!

In fact, if you want to know how to make Mediterranean food, then this new e-book - "The 30-minute Mediterranean diet" - gives you the answers to many important questions and challenges every Mediterranean dieter faces, including:

- How can I succeed with a Mediterranean diet?
- What kind of recipes can I make?
- What are the key principles to this type of diet?
- What are the suggested weekly menus for this diet?
- Are there any cheat items I can make?
  ... and more!

If you're serious about cooking meals on a Mediterranean diet and you really want to know how to make Mediterranean food, then you need to grab a copy of "The 30-minute Mediterranean diet" right now.

Prepare **111 recipes with several ingredients in less than 30 minutes!**

Order at Amazon for only $2,99!

What could be better than a home-cooked meal? Maybe only a Greek homemade meal.

Do not get discouraged if you have no Greek roots or friends.

Now you can make a Greek food feast in your kitchen.

This ultimate Greek cookbook offers you 111 best dishes of this cuisine! From more famous gyros to more exotic Kota Kapama this cookbook keeps it easy and affordable.

All the ingredients necessary are wholesome and widely accessible.

The author's picks are as flavorful as they are healthy. The dishes described in this cookbook are "what Greek mothers have made for decades."

Full of well-balanced and nutritious meals, this handy cookbook includes many vegan options.
Discover a plethora of benefits of Mediterranean cuisine, and you may fall in love with cooking at home.

Inspired by a real food lover, this collection of delicious recipes will taste buds utterly satisfied.

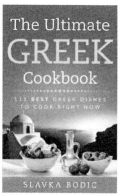

Order at Amazon for only $2,99!

Maybe to try exotic Serbian cuisine?

From succulent sarma, soups, warm and cold salads to delectable desserts, the plethora of flavors will satisfy the most jaded foodie. Have a taste of a new culture with this **traditional Serbian cookbook**.

Order at Amazon for only $2,99!

ONE LAST THING

If you enjoyed this book or found it useful I'd be very grateful if you could find the time to post a short review on Amazon. Your support really does make a difference and I read all the reviews personally, so I can get your feedback and make this book even better.

Thanks again for your support!

Please send me your feedback at

www.balkanfood.org

Printed in Great Britain
by Amazon

79262407R00081